MW01698212

DELIBERATE COACHING

A TOOLBOX FOR ACCELERATING TEACHER PERFORMANCE

Paul Gavoni, EdD   Nicholas Weatherly, PhD

LEARNING SCIENCES INTERNATIONAL

1400 Centrepark Blvd., Ste. 1000
West Palm Beach, FL 33401
717.845.6300
email: pub@learningsciences.com
learningsciences.com

Printed in the United States of America

23 22 21 20 19 1 2 3 4 5

Publisher's Cataloging-in-Publication Data
provided by Five Rainbows Cataloging Services

Names: Gavoni, Paul, author. | Weatherly, Nic, author.

Title: Deliberate coaching : a toolbox for accelerated teacher performance / Paul Gavoni [and] Nic Weatherly.

Description: West Palm Beach, FL : Learning Sciences, 2019.

Identifiers: ISBN 978-1-943920-37-2 (pbk.) | ISBN 978-1-943920-38-9 (ebook)

Subjects: LCSH: Education. | Educational leadership. | School administrators. | Mentoring in education--Handbooks, manuals, etc. | Teachers--Professional relationships. | Educational psychology. | BISAC: EDUCATION / Professional Development. | EDUCATION / Administration / General. | EDUCATION / Educational Psychology. | EDUCATION / Teacher & Student Mentoring.

Classification: LCC LB1731.4 .G38 2019 (print) | LCC LB1731.4 (ebook) | DDC 371.102--dc23.

TABLE OF CONTENTS

ACKNOWLEDGMENTS

As parents, educators, and practitioners, we have a great deal of respect for the educational system. We have been lucky enough to work for and with some tremendous people in both public and private schools throughout our careers. We have learned a great deal and continue to learn from these experiences. We would like to thank Curtis Harris, Nick Green, and Anika Costa for taking the time to review portions of our manuscript. Their expertise in behavior analysis and education has been invaluable to the writing process and has provided important insights. We would also like to thank Andrew Kieta for his contribution to the book. His description of the Morningside Model and the success of a behavior-analytic approach to education offers a nice example of the impact of behavior analysis on learning outcomes and the lives of our students. We would also like to individually acknowledge some special folks.

Paulie

I have been fortunate to be surrounded by and learn from some amazing people across the fields of education, human services, and combat sports. Whether directly or indirectly, the following list of folks have either provided me an important opportunity or furthered my knowledge and ability as a leader, coach, or as a person. They include: Dr. Alex Edmonds, Bill Tomlinson, Brad "One Punch" Pickett, Bruce Gorman, Chris Frick and family, Din Thomas, Francisco Gomez, Frank Krukauskas, Dr. Jason Ampel, John Taylor, Dr. Jose Marinez-Diaz, Dr. Ken Wagner, Kenny "Deuce" Garner, Joel Garcia, Dr. Kisha Bellande-Francis, Leigh Martin, Luigi "The Italian Tank" Fioravanti, Manuel "Manny" Rodriguez, Mario "Big Hurt" Rinaldi, Mike Brown, Milton Lacroix, Dr. Nic Weatherly, Renato Tavares, Roger Krahl, Dr. Scott Neil, and Dr. Tom Gollery.

To my parents, John and Susan Parry, and Paul Gavoni, thank you for teaching me to value helping people and always providing unconditional love. And most of all, thank you to my wife, Nikki Gavoni, and my son, Niko Gavoni, for their constant support along this marvelous journey.

Nic

Any joy and success I experience in my personal and professional lives are because of the support and guidance I get from my lovely wife, Allison, and the inspiration and love I receive from my brilliant and beautiful daughter Emma. I would like to thank the faculty, staff, and students of Western Michigan University with whom I worked while studying behavior analysis for the first time and the team of faculty, staff, and students at the Florida Institute of Technology that continue to research and apply the type of valuable behavioral tools needed to impact the world. I particularly would like to thank Jacqueline Noto for her review of manuscript citations and coaching literature, Joshua Addington and Nicole Adriaenssens for their assistance gathering references, and Chad Kinney, Dennis Uriate, Nelmar Cruz, CC Caberlon, Kayce Nagel, Taylor Hetherington, Noell Jankowski, Estefania Alarcon, and the rest of Florida Tech's Behavioral Leadership Lab for their assistance analyzing and refining coaching concepts. I would also like to thank Dr. Paulie Gavoni for helping me continue to expand my appreciation for the science behind coaching and the application of these principles in a way that has been a great value to my research and practice and, in turn, something I hope will continue to benefit those I serve over the years.

FOREWORD

Leadership is NOT about being in charge. Leadership is about taking care of those in your charge.

—Simon Sinek

Congratulations, you made it through the years of preparation, the interview gauntlet, and you're a school leader. Now what?

From the hiring of new teachers and supporting those new hires, to getting veteran teachers to change their ways, to refereeing conflicts between parents, teachers, and students, to taking aim at what seems like insurmountable district student achievement targets, school leadership is a tough, demanding, sometimes frightening job.

To be successful, you must tackle some Herculean things like improving the school culture, instilling proven high-yield instructional strategies in each classroom, and increasing student achievement levels throughout the campus, just to name a few. Why are some school leaders successful, yet many others are not? Is it luck? Are some just dealt a better hand than others, a better school, better skilled teachers, better kids? Or maybe it's just the innate abilities of a school leader to get people to do things they haven't done before? Nope, none of these are the reason for success. As the character Ron Burgundy in the movie *Anchorman* says, "It's science" . . . and in this case, it's behavioral science!

Dr. Gavoni's and Dr. Weatherly's book, *Deliberate Coaching*, lays it out in a straightforward scientific approach to getting the results all school leaders desire through behavioral science. The success of any school is clearly not born out of luck; rather, the pathway to your arrival at that destination is through a deliberate, systemic, scientific approach. The toolbox for this journey is found in this book. While it may be true that some schools are more challenging to lead than others, through this scientific approach, results can be realized for all.

Setting the table for building school culture, trust, pride, and an expectation of "success through support" begins right in the initial job interview. I've always told school leaders I've worked with that interviewing and hiring is the second most important thing you do (I'll tell you *the* most important later!). Given today's teacher shortages, particularly at high-poverty, low-performing schools, strong teacher applicants clearly have the upper hand; it is a buyer's market with teachers having choice as to where they elect to work. Therefore, directly out of the gate at the interview, I *have* to sell my school, and more importantly, I have to guarantee the teacher's success. Support is the first thing a new applicant wants to hear. Tell your applicant what that support will look like and that you'll ensure his or her success.

For example, immediately after offering a job to a new rookie teacher, I, tongue-in-cheek, would share a prediction: "One afternoon in late September you are going to come to my office and ask to shut the door. Your chin is going to start to wobble, eyes are going to well up, and you are going to say the phrase that every school leader dreads hearing: 'This is not what I thought it was going to be like. I can't do this, I'm going to resign.'" I then ask the new hire to promise right there, at the end of the interview, well before this emotional "late September" moment, that he or she is not going to quit!

As educators, we've all been there. As a first-year teacher, I was there. As a first-year principal, I certainly was there. Let's face it, teacher prep programs and school leader prep programs lack the real "boots on the ground" experiences that are much needed. The "I never learned how to deal with this in college" is too often heard on school campuses. But what I need to drive home with that new hire is that *I promise* to support, coach, and mentor him or her to success. "You will be successful" is my overriding theme.

First-time formal classroom evaluations are always feared by new teachers. I always say, right up front, that mine are not to be feared. If the teacher falls short of expectations in his or her first observation, we simply throw out the evaluation and I train the teacher, I coach the teacher, I model for the teacher . . . and when he or she is ready, only when he or she is ready, we reschedule a do-over. The A and the C of the ABCs of behavioral science are set . . . It now is my job, with tools, like those found in *Deliberate Coaching*, to coach the desired behaviors that bring about the teacher's success and ultimately schoolwide success!

Delivering on that support and coaching teachers to success is undoubtedly *the most* important thing a school leader does (I promised I'd tell you what #1 was!). Coaching teachers to success is a full-time job. Student achievement, which is the school leader's "product" and what he or she will be judged on, will only increase if the leader supports and takes the time to coach teachers to increase their effectiveness. The only way to legitimately increase student achievement is to increase teacher effectiveness. Increased teacher effectiveness leads to increased student achievement. Period, end of story, roll credits! Teacher effectiveness will only increase through a campuswide culture of collegial coaching, trust that breeds risk taking, nonevaluative conversations about effective instructional practices, and, just when you think you're all done, more coaching. That coaching comes from a variety of sources like school leaders, academic coaches, peer coaches, and even personal reflection. It shows itself in the form of frequent, timely feedback. Schools should share these leadership tasks with aspiring leaders and other veteran teachers to grow a supportive coaching community; sharing that leadership will breed even greater returns! My T-shirt says: Envision, Support, Coach, Give Feedback, Repeat. What does your T-shirt say?

So, school leaders, chart the course and take the wheel. School leadership is not for the faint of heart. Have the courage, as Peter Senge said, "to get people to go where they might not have gone themselves." To get there, leaders need to provide the compelling why, the inviting pathway to success, and the desired rewards for arriving at the envisioned destination. The root cause for successfully getting there is found in behavioral science and must not to be left to chance. "It's science," it's the science of coaching, it's *Deliberate Coaching*! Go forth, be fearless, be deliberate. Comfort the challenged, and challenge the comfortable. Take care of those in your charge . . . Coach 'em!

I wish you all the best on your journey to success.

—John Lynch, Turnaround Principal,
Principal Coach, District Leader

FOREWORD

Luck favors the prepared mind. This is a paraphrase of a quote from the famous scientist Louis Pasteur. Pasteur was a microbiologist and chemist, but first and foremost, he was a scientist. And he understood the logic and principles of the scientific method. Although, for example, the fields of psychology, biology, physics, and applied behavior analysis differ in their approaches to studying the natural world, the tenets of the scientific method are applied in the same fashion across these disciplines. The concept of luck or chance in relation to preparation really refers to gauging the probability of success. And it is well known that the probability of success increases as one puts in the effort, focus, and preparation for achieving a particular task. Although the probability of success may increase, how much it increases really hinges on the quality of that preparation.

As a means to ensure that all angles of quality preparation are addressed, the concept of deliberate practice was developed. Deliberate practice essentially refers to the deliberate focus on a specific task by deconstructing the task and practicing each component until efficiency is achieved while receiving steady feedback and increasing the intensity of the practice each time through. In the current text, the authors delineate the steps and techniques required to assume the highest quality preparation that is likely to lead to the most favorable results. This can be at the individual, group, or organizational level.

With that said, the emphasis of the text is focused on coaching, more specifically, Deliberate Coaching. Deliberate Coaching is an expansion of the idea of deliberate practice. The coaching component in any context should *not* be overlooked and is too often underutilized. The importance of quality coaching cannot be overstated. In sport, for example, at the highest levels one can observe the best receiving steady streams of coaching. Michael Jordan in his prime was still being coached and always considered himself a student of the game. The best will always say there's always room for improvement. This premise is true at the educational level as well. Why? Because there are goals to be achieved. Just like it's a sport team's ultimate objective to win, it's a school's objective to win too. Winning for school is likely to entail achievement at the student level, but also at the teacher and administrative levels as well. And success or the probability to succeed improves by applying the tried-and-true strategies—Deliberate Coaching, for example.

It's important to note that because a tried-and-true strategy was used doesn't always mean the results will be optimized. If that is the case, then one should look at the delivery. In research, this is referred to as fidelity. A remedy for this, as the authors delineate, is to be precise, purposeful, and systematic. These are the process measures or cues for executing a particular strategy, again to ensure fidelity, and to enhance or improve the likelihood of success. Quality preparation! And the best way to do this is through the alignment of the system. The authors emphasize the point that all systems must be aligned, which includes all school personnel getting on board.

In any particular field, it's easy to get lost in the jargon that often can get reduced to buzzwords and then ignored or overlooked. Antecedents, reinforcers, shaping, pinpointing, etc., to name a few, are all critical elements and cannot be overlooked, particularly by the individual with the coach's hat. Understanding these concepts, applying these concepts, reapplying these concepts, and adjusting these strategies are all critical in delivering quality coaching. And lastly, do not get hung up on the dichotomy of outcomes. Keep in mind that in the end there is no such thing as success or failure, win or loss, good or bad. There is a continuum and the results fall somewhere on the line, and the goal is to move it in the desired direction. Prepare and luck will favor your hand.

—W. Alex Edmonds, PhD, BCB,
Educational Psychologist and Biofeedback Practitioner

PREFACE

If you want to teach people a new way of thinking, don't bother trying to teach them. Instead, give them a tool, the use of which will lead to new ways of thinking.

—R. Buckminster Fuller

With more than half a century of collective knowledge and experience between us, we are very excited to provide an effective and efficient process to instructional leaders, coaches, or any other professionals with the goal of helping teachers be successful. This process has been at the root of our success across multiple industries. We have used it to accelerate individual, group, and organizational performance in business and education. It has helped CEOs of Fortune 500 companies to achieve fiscal growth and positive culture change. It has helped school leaders to turn around failing schools. It has helped children with disabilities to communicate, teachers to improve instructional performance, and principals to make their schools better. It has even helped professional mixed martial artists to achieve world championship titles. In fact, this process can be used within any field, anywhere, to help people, groups, and organizations achieve positive outcomes. "What," you might be thinking, "could this process be? And if it's so great, why haven't I heard of it?"

The success of this process is based on a proven foundation, and we're going to use that foundation to build tools that you can use to accelerate and maintain teacher performance. That foundation is the science of human behavior, also known as applied behavior analysis (ABA). You might be familiar with some of its principles. Maybe you've read a few things on positive reinforcement or B. F. Skinner. Maybe you've heard people talk about "behavior-based safety" or "fluency training." Or maybe you or someone close to you has a family member diagnosed with autism or a developmental disability, and you've seen the impact behavior analysis has had on those individuals and families. Although behavior analysis has had a long history of success in clinical and business settings, the science of behavior is applicable everywhere there is behavior. We're going to introduce a process that optimizes teacher performance using the science of behavior.

But before we do, let's discuss why teaching and coaching based on science is a good thing. Our goal is to help school leaders and other stakeholders maximize the impact of precious time spent with educators and staff. To do this, we will need to break down some language barriers that might prevent educators from benefiting from its applications. Terminology is a good example. How many times have you been to the doctor, talked to a professor, or listened to the news and thought, "OK . . . now give it to me in English"? Although the science of behavior is vast and sometimes complex, its foundation can be applied by anyone, and because we all impact our environments, we do it every day whether we know it or not. You can't throw a ball up without gravity pushing it back down. And you can't build behavior without the laws of behavior.

Because many consider themselves lay behaviorists in a sense, some of the terminology has become mainstream. You might have heard phrases like "the power of positive reinforcement," and you undoubtedly know what rewards are. If you've read books like *Punished by Rewards* by Alfie Kohn, then you might believe reinforcement and rewards are the same thing, or that "extrinsic" (external) rewards are the cornerstone of ABA. But that's not the case. Reinforcement comes during or after behavior, making it *contingent* (i.e., if this behavior occurs, then a valued outcome will follow) on the behavior. This means it's specific for that behavior, delivered as immediately as possible for that particular behavior. The goal when applying the science of behavior to your school is to enable educators to find what they value as a reinforcer in their day-to-day work so that they are at their best without requiring a lot of external consequences. You want to build good teacher habits, just as a leader or coach wants to build their own good coaching habits. An effective coach helps people find these things through their coaching interactions. "It seemed like you had a good lesson and are in a pretty good mood. What did you do differently today than the last time we spoke?" This is important, as naturally occurring reinforcement is the ultimate goal.

Along these lines, we'll be talking a lot about consequences, positive and negative. The word "consequence" might lead you to think in terms of good and bad, and it may leave you with a bad taste in your mouth. And it should. This is what 99.9 percent of the population outside of the field of ABA thinks. However, in the field, positive simply means something is "added" as a result of behavior. Similarly, negative simply means something is "subtracted" as a result of behavior. We will elaborate more about this later, but trust us when we say that "borrowed" terms like these have led to much confusion, especially when folks believe they are applying positive reinforcement.

Similarly, many people believe what's rewarding or punishing for one person is the same for others. For example, a young child receiving candy for getting an answer right is likely to experience this as a reinforcing consequence. What about sending the disruptive child to detention? Everyone hates that, right? But what if we told you detention might also serve as a reinforcing consequence under the right conditions?

Because of a fundamental misunderstanding of behavior, a variety of concepts have been put forth in attempts to explain its phenomena. In the last few decades there have been a number of authors who have promoted concepts to help with self-improvement, behavior improvement, and performance improvement. For example, it's not unusual for educators to suggest that a student (or staff member) "show more grit," focus on developing a "growth mindset," improve "emotional intelligence," or increase "mindfulness." If you are familiar with these terms or even embrace them, you will be pleased to know that there is one common thread connecting them and many others. That's right, the science of human behavior. And understanding this science will help you further understand and even effectively develop or apply these concepts. Let's take a look at the connection between behavior and these concepts:

- *Grit.* In the *Journal of Personality and Social Psychology*, Duckworth (2007) defined grit as perseverance and passion toward long-term goals. From a behaviorist perspective, grit is goal-directed *behavior* maintained under specific conditions over a period of time. Grit is directly proportionate to the complexity or adversity of conditions required to endure (continue behaving in a specific way toward) a challenge or reach a *performance* goal. Grit can be systematically developed through a process known as *behavioral shaping*.
- *Growth Mindset.* People who believe their talents can be developed through input, hard work, and smart choices have a growth mindset (Dweck, 2017). They tend to achieve more than those who believe their talents are innate. From a behaviorist perspective, talent is overrated. Behaviorists understand that *behavior* and *performance* can be improved as successful approximations are reinforced. Further, people don't simply "believe" anything. As you will see in this book, their beliefs depend on their history of experiences. Think about it. If you *behave* in ways that have led to success in the past, you are more likely to *behave* in those ways again so that you can achieve similar success. As a result, you begin believing in your talents (*behaviors*). Similarly, if you have a history of *behaving* in ways that lead to poor outcomes, then you will believe you're unable to accomplish the

tasks associated with those outcomes. Your "belief" is a result of your past *behavior* and outcomes, not vice versa.

- *Emotional Intelligence.* Popular author Daniel Goleman suggests that emotional intelligence is composed of four domains, including self-awareness, self-management, social awareness, and relationship management. This might have been better termed "behavioral intelligence," as the four domains are made up of *behavior*. Self-management is simply managing one's own *behavior*. Social awareness is being a good observer of the *behaviors* of others and the impact of your *behaviors* on them. Relationship management is *behaving* in ways that are mutually reinforcing. And self-awareness is being aware of one's own *behavior* and thoughts. You might be thinking, "Wait, thoughts aren't behavior." Well, this is one of those fundamental misunderstandings of ABA. While ABA focuses on measurable behavior that can be observed by others, thoughts are recognized as important phenomena known as private events, or rather *behavior* that can only be observed by the person.
- *Mindfulness. Psychology Today* has defined mindfulness as "a state of active, open attention on the present." Supporters of mindfulness recommend strategies like deep breathing, focus on heartbeat, or awareness of thoughts to actively keep attention in the present. Remember, *behavior* includes both the things that other people can observe you doing (e.g., actions that accomplish the task at hand) and things that only you can observe (e.g., heartbeat or thoughts). Mindfulness training has been described as a systematic training of attention and self-control (Tang et al., 2013). From a behaviorist perspective, becoming mindful through mindfulness training requires you to become a good observer (observing is *behavior*!) of one's own *behavior*, the environment, and the impact of your *behavior* on the environment. This includes the environment around you and the environment within you.

As you can see, the above definitions all share a common element: *behavior*! Having a better understanding of behavior as outlined in this book will deepen your knowledge and perhaps application of strategies related to these and many other concepts.

After you've read this book, successfully applied the principles, and used the tools, you will recognize the great need of ABA across almost every facet of experience. Whether you're a parent, teacher, coach, principal, superintendent, CEO, or world leader, a fundamental understanding of the principles of behavior can help you achieve desired outcomes while improving quality of life. We like to think of ABA as the science of helping people. Given its amazing benefits, you will wonder why the science of human behavior hasn't been taught in every teacher and leadership program in the world. This very question has been presented to us as we've shared practical strategies of ABA across the country. In fact, it was after a presentation to school leaders and instructional coaches on practical tools for helping teachers improve performance that we were inspired to write our book.

If you are like the people we've spoken to, you want to make a difference. To that end, you may have purchased the latest coaching book or even received training in a coaching methodology that provided you with various tools. Through our research we've discovered countless definitions of coaching and approaches to coaching. Jim Knight, a well-known author who does research on educational coaching, highlights different types of approaches (Knight, 2009). These include:

1. Instructional coaching
2. Literacy coaching
3. Cognitive coaching
4. Coaching classroom management
5. Content coaching
6. Differentiated coaching
7. Leadership coaching

While many of the definitions and approaches supported by various authors and researchers overlap, some appear contradictory, and not all of them work. As a result, you might be a little hesitant to read this book—as the variety of approaches has already left you in a state of "paralysis by analysis." Like many coaches and instructional leaders, you simply want to help, but you need a clear path and an answer to the question "Where do I start?"

Well, here's some good news. The principles and tools we will share within this book are at the root of any approach or methodology you've read about or received training for. So rather than teaching you something completely different, the information presented here will deepen your knowledge and expand your toolbox regardless of your knowledge and background. If educational coaching were a car, the information we provide might be considered the fuel needed to drive it. Without fuel, even the highest-performing cars won't get past the starting line.

While written for K–12 instructional leaders and coaches, this book is relevant to stakeholders who are invested in the performance improvement of any educator at any level. It is intended to:

- Showcase a practical application of behavior analysis as applied to teachers, school leadership, and education systems
- Make the case for tools based on a proven science by focusing on the concepts, application, and value behind the *Deliberate Coaching* approach.

For ease of reading and clarity of focus, we've divided the book into three sections: (1) "The Current State of Education," (2) "The Science of Behavior," and (3) "The Deliberate Coaching Model."

In "The Current State of Education," we talk about why too many schools have a revolving door of turnover where teachers and leaders come and go inside of a few years. The good news is that we have the methodology; we can improve the system. And the science outlined in this book provides the path.

If you are well aware of the revolving door in education and some of its root causes, you might want to skip to "The Science of Behavior" to dive deeper into the principles behind performance change. We highly recommend that you read this chapter. Understanding the *why* will motivate you and provide you with knowledge you'll need to understand the idiosyncrasies of performance improvement.

But if you wish to get right to the part where we bring research to practice, feel free to skip directly to "The Deliberate Coaching Model." Here we illustrate practical concepts and provide simple tools that will allow you to begin your journey toward accelerating teacher performance.

The power of positive reinforcement, making good things happen when people do good work, is not only for accelerated learning and performance. People like it when good things happen. Coaches find what people value and give them a path to that. The reward doesn't have to be money or tangible items. Sometimes it's simply recognition. Sometimes it's seeing a child succeed because of what they did. Sometimes it's making their job easier. Further, what's reinforcing for one person might not be reinforcing for another person. Coaches find potential reinforcers and promote positive workplace environments, using these reinforcers to build teacher performance and support teachers. Coaches link their coaching to these reinforcers to show the value of their leadership. Nobody wants people to listen to them simply because they have authority or firing power. Leaders want to be respected. Leaders want to be valued. Leaders want trust because their direct reports see that what they say works.

For the school leaders reading this book, we'd like to thank you, on behalf of your teachers, for continuing a journey to support your colleagues. One of the goals of Deliberate Coaching is to get a conversation going at your school. Maybe you'll share it with your colleagues. Maybe you'll even share it with your supervisors. While our approach is based on scientific studies of learning and performance, our real emphasis is on developing a supportive school culture. We want teachers to enjoy teaching because we need good teachers. We want school leaders to enjoy leading teachers because we need good leaders. We want administrators and district decision-makers to enjoy their jobs because we need people from the top fighting for our educators.

We hope that you all will see the value in our approach to teacher management. Integrating a coaching system into your school takes leadership from a reactive mindset—waiting to put out fires—to a more proactive and ongoing method of supporting teachers. You don't want to wait until something is wrong to engage your staff. This will only demonstrate that you care just enough to show up when, in their minds, they've screwed up. Similarly, we hope to show you how you can provide some quick check-ins to see how you can help instead of the teachers only receiving some sort of feedback or support during their scheduled teacher evaluation. Teachers should be provided support when things are working so they know what's working. They'll still need help when things go wrong, but they're almost always doing more things right than wrong, so finding this balance is critical.

But this book isn't just for school management. The "leaders" of the school can be anyone, so coaches can be anyone. They can be principals, vice principals, counselors, peer leaders, anyone that can have an impact on teacher and staff performance. This book is designed to promote positive school cultures that support teachers by capitalizing on every team member at your school. Educators offer an invaluable contribution to our society, and ongoing support can help give them the level of ongoing recognition they deserve. We hope that this book can be the beginning of this process. Moreover, the coaching approach offered in this book is designed to give you a path to integrating science-based strategies into your day as a leader and teacher support. You can start small, changing a few things at a time, but the goal is to find what works given the demands of your school. These things will make a difference, and that difference can make a significant impact on the performance of your teachers and students. The school year is not very long, so it's important to start strong, be consistent, and end stronger!

SECTION 1

THE CURRENT STATE OF EDUCATION

CHAPTER 1

SYSTEMS AND SYSTEMATIC APPROACHES

Science is the captain, and practice the soldiers.

—Leonardo da Vinci

Each of us operates in a number of systems each day. Our homes are systems, containing different people, different duties (fun and chores and more), and different outcomes. Our communities are made up of systems, different groups of people with different resources working together to achieve a common objective. And every school is a system. Schools enroll students into their systems to work with the teachers, staff, administrators, curricula, and resources. It is the job of the people and processes within your school system to produce students with strong learning repertoires that lead to achievement of standards. Each person in the system is valuable and linked in some way to this overall outcome of student success. We all work together to meet our goals.

In short, an educational system can be thought of as a macrosystem (the big umbrella) made up of a number of organizations (e.g., districts and schools) where hundreds of different processes are made up of thousands of different tasks and are accomplished through thousands of different behaviors that must occur daily in order to accomplish a desired outcome: student achievement. Does that sound complex? It is! And these behaviors are contingent upon one another and must be supported at varying levels. For example, the district leader supports the school leaders; the school leaders support the teachers; and the teachers support the students. As you can see from this example, there are many interlocking behaviors that must occur across a variety of positions for students to be successful. In the behavioral literature these interlocking behaviors are known as metacontingencies (Malott, 2003).

So what's all this talk about interlocking behaviors and metacontingencies? Think of it as a car assembly with a series of if-thens. Each person working on the assembly line has a task to complete. *If* that person completes the task according to standard, *then* the next person is ready to complete the next task. In the end, the aggregate product of this combination of tasks (process) is a vehicle ready for the sales force.

The processes in education are much the same. But instead of assembly line workers, the educational system is made up of a variety of professionals ranging from politicians, provosts, and deans and professors in higher education to district leaders, school leaders, guidance counselors, and teachers whose sole purpose is improving student achievement. And these processes occur at the federal, state, and local levels. Ellis and Magee (2007) outline the following as prominent hierarchal units that comprise the educational system:

- Federal agencies creating laws (ensuring implementation of state directives based on federal guidelines)
- State education agencies prescribing educational teaching programs
- School districts providing qualification guidelines for hiring teachers
- Schools (in site-based management systems) hiring teachers
- Classroom teachers implementing the prescribed training programs

According to the current Department of Education's mission statement, the ultimate "aggregate product" of all these interlocking units that make up our educational system is students who are prepared for global competitiveness. Measurement of the educational system can be divided into three categories (OECD, 1998):

- Output indicators (e.g., student achievement measures)
- Attainment indicators (e.g., graduation rates)
- Impact indicators (e.g., percentage of graduates employed at a certain job level)

And of course, leading indicators (think mile markers and signs that let you know you're headed in the right direction) along the way inform progress and intervention aimed at improving student achievement. These might include measures of financial and material resources, human resources, and background conditions of the students.

What and How Students Are Taught

When we used the assembly line to illustrate the interconnectedness of various processes, tasks, and behaviors, the metaphor wasn't too far from the truth. Many believe the current model of education in the United States continues to reflect the training mentality where students were taught the essential skills required to become a successful factory worker. In the factory model, students were grouped based on their age, not their abilities. Sound familiar? At that time, factory-working skills were required to be competitive in a global market for the majority of folks who were less affluent. But times have changed dramatically, and the education system has been too slow to catch up. Unfortunately, the longer a system is in place, the harder it is to change.

In 1984, B. F. Skinner published an article titled "The Shame of American Education." In it, he noted that technology capable of doubling the rate of learning in schools across the country had been available for twenty years.

> Recent analyses of American schools and proposals for school reform have missed an essential point: Most current problems could be solved if students learned twice as much in the same time and with the same effort. It has been shown that they can do so (a) when the goals of education are clarified, (b) when each student is permitted to advance at his or her own pace, and (c) when the problem of motivation is solved with programmed instructional materials, so designed that students are very often right and learn at once that they are. The theories of human behavior most often taught in schools of education stand in the way of this solution to the problem of American education, but the proposal that schools of education simply be disbanded is a step in the wrong direction. Teachers need to be taught how to teach, and a technology is now available that will permit them to teach much more effectively. (p. 947)

Now here we are, fifty-five years since that technology has been made available, and we are in a similar boat. But instead of embedding systems that help schools become a better place to teach and learn critical standards, we've simply increased the number of standards being taught, reduced funding for the arts, disregarded the fact that individuals learn at different rates by creating a timeline of expected learning, and developed numerous punitive sanctions to enforce ill-advised policy. This scattershot approach to standards-driven instruction has had a negative impact on the development of fluency (speed and accuracy) in fundamental knowledge and skills.

And fluency is a prerequisite for accelerating performance. Much like an arrow shot by an archer, if fundamental skills are even slightly off in the beginning stages of learning, learners will fall far short of hitting the bull's-eye.

"The entire standards movement is put at risk by those who have replaced focus and meaning with quantity and coverage."
—Doug Reeves

The effectiveness of accelerating performance by systematically developing fundamentals was illustrated well in a study on teaching elementary students to read (Alessi,

1987). The investigator found that by blending (think sounding out letters to make words) only forty or so letter-sound combinations in the English language, a child would be able to read almost five hundred thousand words. Can you imagine the time teachers could save by teaching the forty sounds instead of five hundred thousand words? This concept is rooted in the phenomenon known as adduction (think spontaneous learning), whereby complex learning can emerge without explicit instruction when the right fundamentals are combined, sequenced, and taught to fluency. The systematic development of fluency is critical as it "enables competent individuals to function efficiently and effectively in their natural environments" (Binder, 1996).

Don't take our word for it. Project Follow Through, one of the most extensive educational experiments ever performed by the federal government, compared twenty-two different models of instruction across more than two hundred thousand children and 178 communities composed of students from diverse demographic, ethnic, and socioeconomic backgrounds (Engelmann, 2007). The results were clear: direct instruction (DI), a research-based approach to instructional design and implementation rooted in behavior analysis (Binder & Watkins, 1990), had a significantly higher impact on academic achievement than any of the other programs. Students participating in the research also demonstrated higher self-esteem and self-confidence than students who received different models of instruction. Follow-up research found that students who received DI:

- continued to outperform their peers
- were more likely to finish high school
- were more likely to pursue higher education

Oh, and by the way, this research was originally conducted between 1968 and 1979. Yet here we sit, forty years after these amazing outcomes were established, and direct instruction, what one professional called the "dirty little secret from the biggest education study ever" (Lindsay, 2014), is only being used in a handful of schools.

The question you are likely asking is, "Why, oh why, oh why aren't major changes within the educational system happening?" Unfortunately, the answers are deep, varied, and beyond the scope of this book. However, we will take a brief shot at one or two potential reasons below, and then further reflect on them in future chapters.

The first has to do with systematic change management. While studies like Project Follow Through yield amazing data, research by its nature is conducted by researchers, not change agents. Approaches to getting people to embrace and engage in change is often a long and sometimes challenging process that has been documented in volumes of literature by a plethora of authors and practitioners. In John P.

Kotter's popular book *Leading Change*, published in 1996, Kotter highlighted eight errors in organizational change:

1. Allowing too much complacency
2. Failure to create a sufficiently powerful guiding coalition
3. Underestimating the power of vision
4. Undercommunicating the vision
5. Permitting obstacles to block the new vision
6. Failing to create short-term wins
7. Declaring victory too soon
8. Neglecting to anchor changes firmly in the corporate culture

It's easy to imagine that all or most of these errors might be partially responsible for the absence of direct instruction in most schools across our nation.

The second reason has to do with habit. You've probably heard the saying "You can't teach an old dog new tricks." Well, one might consider the educational system the old dog and direct instruction the new trick. The longer a system has been in place, the harder it is to change—that is, if you aren't familiar with the science of human behavior as applied to organizations. We'll talk more about behaviorism's underlying principles in future chapters. For now, suffice it to say that there was clearly little to no science behind the delivery of direct instruction to the masses. Had there been, we likely wouldn't have written this book.

We can do better. Instead of trying to enforce policy through threat of punishment, where behavior decreases because of something undesired following the behavior, we must seek to systematically transfer the most effective practices for learning. The technology for accelerating the acquisition of knowledge and skills exists, and it should be taught to fluency in higher education so that it can be effectively transferred into the classroom.

Case Example: The Systematic Application of Behavior Analysis

Promises are a dime a dozen in education, but guarantees are rare. It's hard to imagine a school that guarantees student growth, let alone one that is willing to put money on the line. Seattle's Morningside Academy does just that, guaranteeing two years of growth in a student's area of greatest need or fully refunding their tuition. In nearly forty years, less than 1 percent of tuition has been refunded. Take a look at the average Morningside Academy Student Grade Level Growth in Reading Comprehension during the 2015–2016 school year. Jaw-dropping to many.

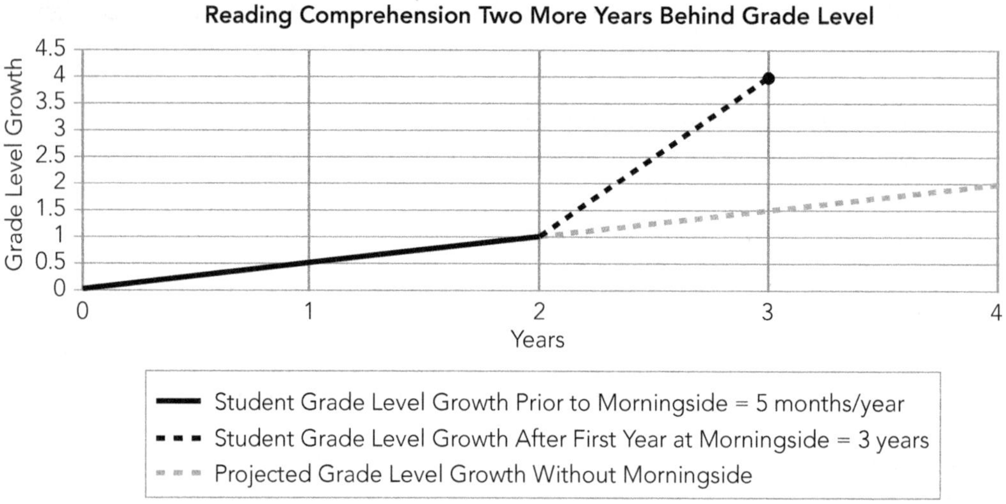

Figure 1.1. Average student grade level growth per year in the area of reading comprehension for students who were two or more years below their grade level prior to entering Morningside Academy; their projected growth without the Morningside intervention; and their actual growth at the end of the year. These data reflect growth on the Iowa Tests of Basic Skills (ITBS) for the 2015–16 school year.

What makes this possible? The answer is a comprehensive learning model based on mountains of research on what works in education. In 1980, Dr. Kent Johnson founded Morningside Academy, a behaviorally based laboratory school that helps elementary and middle school students catch up and get ahead. Inspired by John Dewey's laboratory schools, Morningside serves tier II general education and mild special education students—the forgotten 40 percent of students in the United States. These kids present with a broad range of learning disabilities and far too often fall through the cracks of the American education system.

The success of children at Morningside is the outcome of years of research and development into the Morningside Model of Generative Instruction (MMGI), a generic learning model that has produced profound results for a wide range of learners. MMGI is based on the evidence-based best practices that have proven effective with learners at the laboratory school and at schools across North America.

MMGI is built on five pillars. First, research-based curriculum is selected that focuses on specific component skills. Morningside instructional designers examine the types of "holistic" and "real-world" activities that often take place in today's general education classrooms. Then, they select and design instructional programs that will best teach the component skills that students need to be successful in those general education settings.

Second, students are placed in classes by what they can and can't do, rather than by their age. This process of homogeneous achievement grouping allows for optimal instructional groups and facilitates the rapid growth that students at Morningside make. After selecting the best curriculum and placing students in the best learning environments, Morningside teachers directly and explicitly teach components using *mathetics*, the underlying science of direct instruction. Teachers use this science to ensure that students can accurately complete a targeted objective before moving on to new objectives.

The fourth pillar is precision teaching. Once students are accurate in their performance of a newly taught skill or repertoire, they engage in systematic, daily practice in order to build fluency. At Morningside, mastery does not just mean high accuracy, but high accuracy plus high frequency—or speed. Mountains of research show that completing skills in a timely fashion is a key indicator of retention, generalization, and more.

Lastly, Morningside systematically creates learning environments that produce *generativity*—new learning without instruction. The curriculum is arranged in such a way that students can be given new challenges that they will be successful in solving. This means putting them into structured versions of the "holistic" and "real-world" activities that are prominent in general education. The big difference is that Morningside students have shown that they have all of the skills necessary to be successful in these environments that can often be overwhelming. One way this is done is through teaching students problem-solving strategies, such as Talk Aloud Problem Solving, a problem-solving and reasoning curriculum developed by Morningside principal and associate director Joanne Robbins.

The desired outcome of all of this work is generativity: learning new things without instruction. By focusing on critical component skills, guaranteeing mastery via explicit and direct instruction, using precision teaching to ensure fluency, and systematically arranging learning environments, students at Morningside are consistently put into positions where they find they can do something they've never been directly taught.

A common challenge from Morningside teachers is "I bet you can figure that out on your own!" And nothing builds intrinsic motivation and drive better than doing just that. It's clear that students cannot possibly learn everything they'll ever need to know in the relatively short time they spend in school, so helping them construct repertoires that allow them to meet ever-changing demands is critical to their long-term success. Focusing on prerequisite component skills—which are far too often overlooked—and teaching problem-solving and reasoning strategies yields agile, confident, persistent learners.

Labels do not and should not define children. Rather than trying to compensate for or work around learning challenges, MMGI uses a scientific approach to directly target and strengthen those areas. Forty years of data support this view, and Morningside shows no sign of slowing down. MMGI continues to be developed, helping the next generation of students build the repertoires they need to be successful learners and citizens.

Behavior analysis offers science and tools behind learning and performance. If someone is learning, it's because of the laws of behavior, whether or not those laws are being acknowledged or properly utilized. The more you know about this science and the tools offered from behavior analysis, the greater control you can have on the learning environment. The evolution of educational systems could really maximize learning by finding ways to embed science-based teaching practices in schools....and *coaching* those teaching with these practices to support them!

CHAPTER 2

STATE OF EDUCATION

The man who moves a mountain begins by carrying away a small stone.

—Confucius

Behavior analysis can offer tons of evidence-based tools that have proven to be effective at improving a range of employee behaviors in countless settings. But these tools will only work if they can be integrated correctly into your particular school. Your school has goals specific to your school, a staff infrastructure that works for your school, and a long history of what's been working and what hasn't been working. Evaluating the state of education over time will leave you to consider a number of factors and potential barriers that can stand in the way of long-term improvements. Every school has a certain number of people responsible for the performance of teachers, and the number of these individuals will have an impact on how much time is available to shape and maintain teacher performance. It's not the job of school leadership to simply *evaluate* performance. School leaders are in a position to help *build* the type of teacher performance that will lead to the outcomes and culture necessary to hit your goals. But whether they assign a principal, vice principal, counselor, or even district coach for added support, there are a number of things that need to be done and only so many hours in the day. If you can't find a way to overcome these constraints, then leadership strategies might be left to trainings, evaluations, and putting out fires instead of proactively building and supporting teacher performance.

Time is money, and funding is always an issue when it comes to finding staff for coaching and resources for trainings and support systems. Whether you're making the case for funding at the district level or trying to manage the funds at the school level, this is a barrier that can get in the way of any leadership engagement. The solution isn't to ignore consistent support in favor of quick training options; finding efficient ways to integrate your coaching system is a critical initial step.

In the current state of education, policy makers have focused on desired outcomes and not as much on how to get those outcomes. This is a slippery slope that leads to ignoring critical life and academic skills and instead fixates on, for example, answers on standardized tests.

Tale of Two Classrooms

Mr. Kohn has been a teacher for twenty years and has an approach that seems to work for him. Students aren't very active during his class, but they maintain adequate test scores with a few instances of minor student disruptions each week. While the test scores aren't exactly the highest in of the district, they're enough to get by. Students who perform at a high level are left alone. Students who act out or perform at a lower level get more attention.

Mr. Skinner's classroom runs a bit differently. He's been there a few years less, but he's managed to gain quite a reputation for turning out productive students who speak highly about his methods. He monitors progress and pays attention to how many opportunities each student has to engage in activities throughout the day. Some students like certain activities more than others, and he uses information on their preferences to keep them motivated. His students say that learning is fun, good things happen when they're learning. They're never bored. They seem to consistently go above and beyond minimum expectations.

So what's the key difference in what they're doing? Mr. Skinner focuses on behaviors, not just outcomes. He focuses on engagement, ensuring that each student gets ample opportunities to succeed. High-performing students shouldn't be ignored because they seem fine on their own. All students deserve opportunities to grow, all students have unique needs, and all students have their own likes and dislikes. You need high-achieving students, but it's the way you get there that offers the critical opportunity for growth.

The Blame Game

While some schools can tout high achievement, too many struggle with making desired achievement gains. When this happens, the blame game begins. Policy makers blame and pressure state leadership; state leadership blames and pressures districts; district leadership blames and pressures school leadership; school leadership blames and pressures teachers. As this happens, students fail to reach their potential as frustrated parents blame the teachers; frustrated teachers begin pointing their fingers back at the parents; and leadership on every level receives the finger until it bounces back to policy makers. Policy makers under pressure decide they need to do something, so they draft a new policy and begin the whole blame game again.

The blame game is real. And it's painful for all involved. Let's take a closer look at an all-too-common scenario in failing schools:

> After graduating from college, a group of first-year teachers is hired by a hopeful principal of a Title I school. She was assigned to the school after the former principal was fired by the district because the school failed to make adequate gains three years in a row. The principal wants seasoned and culturally diverse teachers, but high-poverty schools in her area have a bad reputation, so her selection pool is thin. The group of teachers begins the school year aspiring to help students in poverty achieve.
>
> While the first week isn't so bad, seemingly small issues begin to wear. In the second week, most begin struggling. Lesson planning, grading, managing student behavior, and instructing based on the district's evaluation model quickly erodes their morale. Their high hopes and aspirations are replaced with stress that progressively evolves into panic as the principal walks through the classrooms, pressuring them to boost student achievement. Attempting to help, the principal leaves each with a to-do list for improving instructional practices.
>
> The new teachers make it through the first quarter. While they have been assigned mentors, most are too busy struggling in their own classrooms to provide much guidance. Those who did receive guidance and tried some of the suggested techniques aren't getting the desired outcomes. Many in the group are now questioning their career choices. What seemed to be the first steps toward a life's dream have rapidly disintegrated into a nightmare.
>
> While they put their tough faces on, many cry at home and are anxious about coming into school each morning. A few actually break down crying to the principal. The principal, while sympathetic to their plight, is receiving flak from the district as achievement scores aren't where they should be. Asking for support, the district provides the school with two instructional coaches who each serve five other schools. One of the coaches is a reading coach; the other is a math coach who has some background in classroom management.
>
> After meeting with the principal to identify the group of teachers in need, the coaches observe and complete individual checklists

> to rank fifty instructional and classroom-management practices as "Not in Place," "Somewhat in Place," and "In Place." They then debrief with one another to determine the best approach for helping targeted teachers. Some of the teachers scored an "In Place" on a couple of the targeted elements; however, most of the elements are "Somewhat in Place" or "Not in Place." The reading coach thinks the problem is classroom management, while the math coach blames most of the issues on instructional strategies related to reading.
>
> Failing to reach a compromise on what high-impact instructional behaviors should be targeted, they use a scattershot approach, identifying thirty-five out of the fifty elements that require improvement. They hand the checklist to the principal, then inform her they won't be back until next week.
>
> The end of the year rolls around. The principal is tired and many of the teachers have said they won't be returning. District leadership, unhappy with student achievement and teacher attrition, decides the principal wasn't a good match for the school and hires another one in her place.
>
> The new principal, enthusiastic and optimistic, seeks to hire seasoned and culturally diverse teachers; however, she struggles because high-poverty schools in her area have a bad reputation, so her selection pool is thin. She ends up hiring a group of first-year teachers to fill her remaining positions. The new teachers begin the school year aspiring to help students in poverty achieve … and the blame game, like Groundhog Day, begins again.

This story is like a bad movie, except that students and educators can't walk out of the theater and ask for a refund. Too many are stuck. If you've not experienced this as an educator or even a student, consider yourself fortunate. Many educators in struggling schools feel like they're rowing upstream. They soon fatigue and leave at the expense of themselves and our children. Michelle Obama echoed the sentiments of many when she stated, "A child's course in life should be determined not by the zip code she's born in."

A personal reflection on the state of education in your region, state, or nation will most likely lead you to find opportunities for improvement. There are many ways we can improve education, some of which we hit on in the book and some that extend far beyond it. While it's important to vote, get involved with the school board, and find other ways to make changes within various levels of your school system, this book will hopefully show you how to provide better support for the valuable personnel who make up the school cultures we send our children to.

The Fight for Knowledge

Cus D'Amato, the famed boxing coach who trained multiple champions including the infamous Mike Tyson, once said, "A boy comes to me with a spark of interest, I feed the spark and it becomes a flame. I feed the flame and it becomes a fire. I feed the fire and it becomes a roaring blaze." This "spark" is fundamental to getting somebody to engage in something. But when people are thrown into deep waters unprepared, their spark is often dowsed. As we've already highlighted, this occurs far too often in education as leaders and teachers are thrown into deep waters, unprepared to meet the demands of the school and classroom.

In the beginning stages of development, the original spark might be enough to get educators moving; however, it is not enough for sustainability. If educators are to succeed, trainers must take great care to purposefully (with intentional design) and systematically develop skills required for them to reach established goals. If the educator is unable to observe meaningful consequences that result from those skill, the skill and the motivation to use them are likely to fade quickly. To ensure that people will accomplish targeted goals and achieve desired outcomes, focus must be placed on what skill sets should be developed and how those skills will be developed.

Behavior = Believing

Valuing goals is part of the formula for successful performance. As such, it is extremely important to involve people in their development whenever possible to increase engagement in schools. However, for the formula to be effective, it is equally as important that educators believe they can perform a given task, believe performing this task will help them achieve the desired results, and believe professional developers and coaches will help them improve their performance. This belief in their ability to accomplish a particular task is what Albert Bandura (1997) termed "self-efficacy" and has been receiving increased attention recently as a predictor of success in relation to both student and teacher success. But belief, regardless of who you are or what you do, is not something that is built by simply telling people they can do something. Belief occurs as a result of behavior. And while believing and having confidence might get somebody to try something, it isn't sufficient for lasting success. It is behavior that achieves meaningful outcomes that ultimately leads to success and "self-efficacy."

In other words, if they repeatedly behave in some way, they are repeatedly able to observe the desired outcome as a result of these "mastery" experiences. As a result, their belief in their ability is strengthened. And if this outcome is valued by the individual, this increases the likelihood that they will continue performing in order to achieve the result. In the end, the goal of training isn't about getting people to believe. The goal here is to develop somebody's skill sets to the point where if they perform a task, they will be successful. And though many struggling educators lack a sense of "self-efficacy" or "belief' in their ability to achieve certain outcomes because they've not yet had these "mastery" experiences, they truly want to be successful. They fight every day for it!

Fighting for Education

Educators are very much like fighters. Instead of arming themselves with combative skills, they arm themselves with knowledge and instructional skills as they battle to empower their students with the repertoire they need to be successful personally and professionally. Telling them what to do or how to do something is insufficient for success. Can you imagine a boxing coach throwing one of his novice fighters into the ring with a professional after simply telling her what they should do and how they should fight? Do you think this would result in the fighter strengthening her skill set or subsequent belief in her ability that results from successful experiences? Do you think the fighter would value him as a coach? Nope. Rather than learning anything, the novice fighter would likely employ whatever skills exist in her current repertoire to avoid taking a beating. Afterward, the novice fighter would probably view the coach as callous. And the fighter might falsely believe she doesn't have what it takes to be a "contenda."

"Knowledge is of no use unless you put it into practice." —Anton Chekhov

We just can't understand why so many teachers and leaders are just thrown into the schools to take a "beating" like the novice fighter. All too often, universities and teacher preparation or induction programs tell them what and how to do what they're supposed to do with the expectation that it will lead them to successfully doing it. This is counterproductive and costly on many levels to the teachers, staff, coaches, leaders, school, and—most of all—students. Skills must be developed through regular practice.

For this reason, it is essential that those associated with training employ systematic strategies for developing skills (using organized plans or repeatable procedures) that will eventually allow educators to perform in a way that leads to a desired outcome. These strategies should focus on strengthening the educator's performance to the point where they can have mastery experiences by systematically developing their declarative, procedural, and conditional knowledge. While the terms for these kinds of knowledge are increasingly popular in education, we like to break them down into their simplest forms: what to do, how to do it, and *when* to do it.

Declarative Knowledge

While *instructing* people on how to do something is insufficient for getting them to perform successfully, it's still an important part of the formula for developing successful performance. In education, understanding what to do is known as declarative knowledge. Declarative knowledge has been described by some as the factual information accumulated (Stürmer, Könings, & Seidel, 2012). This is the "know" associated with learning. And what's a simple way to determine if somebody knows something? Behavior! Specifically, verbal behavior! Can the person communicate the information to us verbally or in writing? One simple way to assess if somebody "knows" what to do is to simply ask them, "What are you supposed to do?" If they can't describe each step, this is a good indicator that they may not know what to do, let alone be able to do it.

When providing the "what," it's also helpful for educators to understand the "why," as this oftentimes directly impacts the "will." Folks who are told to do something that doesn't make sense to them are far less likely to focus on learning it during training or performing it in school. In contrast, folks who are taught to understand the why in the beginning are far more likely to engage in the learning and skill-development process as they come to understand how the skills are linked to meaningful outcomes. You want people to participate because they see value in participating, not simply because they're told to participate.

A good coach who is seeking to develop a teacher's knowledge might say, "Here is why—try it this way (*modeling*) ... What are your thoughts?" It's important to know what your educators are thinking. Their thoughts can act as a formative assessment to guide future development efforts. It will also affect their willingness to participate in future talent development linked to procedural knowledge.

Good coaches frequently test their teachers' knowledge by asking them questions about the skills they're performing—questions like "Why should you ask a question related to a lesson *before* calling on a student as opposed to calling on a student first and *then* asking the question?" The answer in this case is to engage all students in thinking about the question. Calling on one student first and then asking can inadvertently make other students less engaged. Helping the teacher understand this increases the likelihood that they'll ask the question first. They don't want their students to disengage as this can sometimes increase misbehavior and will negatively impact achievement!

Procedural Knowledge

Knowledge acquisition is the core element of many university- and district-based teacher-preparation programs (Darling-Hammond, 2006); however, skill acquisition is too often overlooked. In the education world, knowing how to do something has become known as procedural knowledge. You might consider this the know-how that connects what educators have learned (declarative knowledge) to what they do.

Trainers might initially explain what a teacher should do and why they should do it. However, this consumes a very brief chunk of the time allotted to training. Good trainers develop training regimens and require the teachers they're supporting to build knowledge through practice linked to successful outcomes (e.g., increasing student engagement). By "practice," we mean trainers systematically develop teachers' skills by requiring them to engage in the repetitive rehearsal of those skills. If we wish for any educator to perform successfully within the school, they *must* have the opportunity to practice critical skills to a standard of proficiency.

However, as Vince Lombardi once said, "Practice does not make perfect. Only perfect practice makes perfect." This statement is pretty accurate. In order to perfect a skill, performers must receive feedback. If a performer practices a skill without feedback, they might quickly become very good at a skill that is very bad!

Just like coaches in sports help athletes reach performance goals by creating conditions whereby the athletes become experts in their respective arts, it should be the goal of teacher-preparation, induction programs, and training programs to allow for purposeful and precise practice. And when we talk about precision, we mean providing teachers exactly what they need to be successful in the classroom through targeted training and specificity of feedback.

In chapter 6 we will cover the topic of deliberate practice when teaching skills to children in the classroom. In sports, deliberate practice is the purposeful approach that distinguishes experts from the average Joe. The foundation of this practice is breaking down specific skills and training into chunks and allowing the performer to become fluent through repetition *and feedback*. Good athletes spend hours deliberately drilling the skills of their sport while coaches provide them with a steady stream of feedback about specific skills to shape their performance. Just like these athletes and students, educators *must* engage in rehearsal of a skill *with feedback* if they're going to develop skills to any level of proficiency. Unfortunately, this isn't happening enough.

Clearly one-shot "sit and gets" for educators are not enough. Though trainers in education don't necessarily need to understand the science behind talent development, good trainers understand that talent is progressively developed through multiple learning opportunities that include practice and feedback. But on top of not providing enough practice opportunities, many educational talent development programs often expect their talent to learn too much, too soon.

CHAPTER 3

STATE OF TEACHING AND LEARNING

If you change the way you look at things, the things you look at change.

—Wayne Dyer

Where We Are

Teachers have the power to make a substantial impact on the academic growth, health, and well-being of their students. But this is a tough job, and it comes with a lot of responsibility and stressors. Some studies rank teaching among the most stressful occupations (Johnson et al., 2005). Not only does this reduce morale, attendance, and effectiveness in the classroom (Hakanen et al., 2006), but one study published by the *American Journal of Alzheimer's Disease & Other Dementias* (Lippa, 2013) actually found that teachers are much more likely than other professionals to be diagnosed with progressive speech and language disorders.

Given the stress and health issues, it's not surprising that many teachers are leaving the profession (Jepson & Forrest, 2006). Teacher turnover plagues too many schools and districts. Unfortunately, the immediate effect of teacher turnover in schools is that our children are harmed by poor instruction. This is especially true of high-poverty schools and classrooms serving students with disabilities. Some investigators claim that teacher attrition costs us more than $2.2 billion per year. Still others have conservatively estimated the cost of teacher turnover in American public schools to be $7.3 billion per year (Carroll, 2007). Unfortunately, the problem appears to be getting worse. Researchers project that there will be a teacher shortage of more than one hundred thousand by 2019 (Sutcher, Darling-Hammond, & Carver-Thomas, 2016).

Wading through the first year isn't easy for many teachers. Some are so traumatized, they leave the field altogether. Although the data vary, various studies report that anywhere from 17 to 46 percent of new teachers quit within their first five years. Some researchers found more than 66 percent of teachers who leave come from schools of high poverty (Marinell & Coca, 2013). We've personally witnessed attrition rates at over 80 percent in the most dysfunctional schools—and these rates don't only apply to teachers.

Turnover rates for principals are scary, especially given that principals have been found to impact student achievement by up to 25 percent (Seashore-Louis et al., 2010). Principal attrition ranges from 15 to 30 percent each year, with some studies finding that about 50 percent of principals don't make it past three years (School Leaders Network, 2014), especially in schools serving more low-income, minority, and low-achieving students (Béteille, Kalogrides, & Loeb, 2012, p. 906). As the research would suggest, teachers *and* leaders are coming into the field unprepared to meet the demands of the classroom and school.

How We Got Here

In our opinion, a big problem is that teacher and leader preparation and induction programs are primarily rooted in theory, with little practice and oftentimes zero coaching to help apply skills they learn to the school. We're not suggesting that theory isn't useful, but its utility is limited to the degree it can assist us in understanding the real world in real time. While theories might help us see the big picture, skills are required to link theory to the real-world, real-time applications. In education, this translates to student achievement. Check out the relatively well-known study by Joyce and Showers (2002) regarding the generalization of skills into the classroom after a teacher is only provided theory.

What kind of classroom impact does simply providing theory and demonstrations to teachers have? None! None of the knowledge and skills transferred to practice! It's dismal, but it makes sense. If telling (theory) and showing (demonstration) were all it took for folks to learn, teacher success would be off the charts, and so would student achievement. Unfortunately, this is what too many teachers and leaders are getting. The revolving door of teacher and leader attrition bankrupts organizational memory at the expense of students and taxpayers.

It's no secret that high turnover undermines student achievement. When policy makers conceived the No Child Left Behind Act (NCLB) in 2002, teachers were left dangling in the wind as all eyes shifted toward the effectiveness of instruction in the classroom. High-stakes testing, Adequate Yearly Progress (AYP), and 100 percent proficient demands established measures and goals without much consideration of the knowledge and skills of those required to produce these outcomes. Instead

Why Is Coaching Important?

"Improving teachers' learning—and, in turn, their own practice and their students' learning—requires professional development that is closely and explicitly tied to teachers' ongoing work. Coaching addressess that requirement." (Neufeld and Roper)

Professional Development Outcomes			
Professional Development Elements	**Knowledge Level** (Estimated percentage of participants understanding content)	**Skill Level** (Estimated percentage of participants demonstrating proficiency in the instructional practices)	**Transfer to Practice** (Estimated percentage of participants regularly implementing instructional practices in the classroom)
Theory (e.g., presenter explains content — what it is, why it is important, and how to teach it)	10%	5%	0%
Demonstration (e.g., presenter models instructional practices)	30%	20%	0%
Practice (e.g., participants implement instructional practices during the session)	60%	60%	5%
Coaching (e.g., participants receive ongoing support and guidance when they return to the classroom)	95%	95%	95%

Adapted from Joyce, B., & Showers, B. (2002). *Student achievement through staff development* (3rd ed.). Alexandria, VA: Association for Supervision and Curriculum Development.

Figure 3.1.

of focusing on strategies for developing and accelerating educator performance to improve student achievement, the NCLB simply set high standards for students and then sought to hold schools "accountable" for establishing measurable success. More accurately, they blamed schools for not meeting unreasonable demands.

The assumption seems to have been that teachers weren't getting the job done because they were lazy or incompetent. So to light the proverbial fire under the butts of educators, "wise" policy makers with arguably little educational experience put pen to paper to right the wrongs of the naughty district, school, and classroom leaders. Districts were forced to double down on this by allocating a ton of money and resources toward improving evaluation processes to correct teacher performance.

The result might be best described as a chain reaction:

- Teachers were forced to teach to the test to avoid the ire of the school leader.
- School leaders were compelled to direct teachers' focus toward select "bubble" students who could help schools make the grade.
- District leaders leaned on school leaders to make the necessary gains.
- State leaders pressured district leaders to get the job done.
- High-paid consultants were brought in to guide leadership.
- Technology was purchased and scattershot across districts.

The pressure was so great, it even led some good people to behave poorly, as evidenced by cheating scandals that rocked a variety of districts.

And after all is said and done, even with some promising developments on the horizon, people continue to blame teachers—pushing compliance by wielding accountability like a sword—instead of addressing a few key issues at the root. When students fail, we blame the teacher. When schools fail, we blame the leader. What about those who've failed teachers and leaders? Who is responsible for that? Let's stop blaming and start figuring out how to bring out the best in teachers so they can bring out the best in their students.

Preparation Programs

The reasons for lack of school progress and failure are wide-ranging and debated across industries. However, one issue that seems to get left by the wayside (while teachers and leaders are blamed) is how well teachers and leaders are being prepared for the demands of the classroom. If our students are going to reach their maximum potential, we must seek to bring out the best in teachers and leaders. Teachers in the top 20 percent of performance have been found to generate five to six more months of learning each year than low-performing teachers. And as we noted earlier, school leaders have been found to affect student achievement by as much as 25 percent.

Given the impact of these professionals, it's shocking—to say the least—that many teachers and leaders entering the profession struggle to even pass certification exams. Teachers who transfer into education from another field without adequate preparation are two to three times more likely to leave the field (Ingersoll, Merrill, & May, 2014). And teachers who do not receive induction or mentoring are twice as likely to leave (Smith & Ingersoll, 2004).

Even those who are fortunate enough to receive formal education at a university struggle. According to a report by the US Department of Education (2016), "Far too many teachers say they feel unprepared for the classroom after completing teacher preparation programs". This isn't surprising given that research suggests a clear lack of empirical evidence to support methods used in teacher-preparation programs (Walsh, 2006). Well-known educational researcher John Hattie (2009) hammers this notion home as he recognizes that "There is no set of essential experiences that must be taught, let alone a 'correct' order for teaching students to become teachers."

Researchers investigating school leadership-preparation programs also cite a drastic need for improvements, as they have found a major disconnect between professor knowledge and the actual needs of the schools (Murphy & Vriesenga, 2006).

Teachers and leaders want and deserve better.

None of this is new. The issue has been recognized for decades. In preparation for the needs of the millennium, the American Council on Education (ACE) Presidents' Task Force on Teacher Education developed an action plan. In their words:

> This action plan provides information on improving the quality of education offered to teachers and school leaders, reporting the results of a task force study which found that: student success depends mainly on teacher quality; the essential competencies of effective teachers are command of the subject, preparation in effective pedagogical practice, and high overall academic performance; strong and effective teacher education programs share many common characteristics; the academic capacity of graduates who enter teaching is comparable to that of college graduates overall for prospective secondary teachers, but below average for prospective elementary teachers; teachers are inadequately prepared to understand and apply technology to teaching; current mechanisms of academic quality control are inadequate to ensure that only fully qualified teachers enter teaching; there is an opportunity to transform teacher quality with the hiring of at least 2.5 million teachers in the next decade; special efforts are needed to address shortages in high-poverty schools, special-needs programs, and the sciences, and among minority teachers; and demand for new teachers can be reduced significantly by reducing teacher attrition.

Even the data being collected by many preparation programs are practically worthless when it comes to measuring skill development by students. In research on school leadership preparation in the United States (Murphy & Vriesenga, 2006), researchers found that 80 percent of research on the topic focused on curricula or instructional strategies, which almost exclusively relied on student perception of:

- the degree to which program goals were met
- the extent to which program elements were valuable
- self-worth

And get this. According to the authors, "There are no research articles in the leading journals in the field over the last quarter century that directly assess the skills and knowledge gained in preparation programs," nor are there any articles that measure changes in student performance.

In fact, university-based principal preparation programs have been scrutinized regarding their effectiveness (e.g., Darling-Hammond, 2006; Murphy, Moorman, & McCarthy, 2008). Some researchers even suggest that the lack of leadership preparation programs is at the root of many issues across the nation's education system (Levine, 2005).

This is significant and echoed in the Wallace Foundation's (2008) report, which indicates that the school principal is the number one person for ensuring that quality instruction is provided across the school.

Given the research and data above, coupled with our personal experiences, it's safe to say that many school leaders are in the same boat as teachers in that they're inadequately prepared to meet the leadership demands of the schools they serve.

Like a novice boxer who's thrown into the ring with a prizefighter to see if they've got what it takes, leaders and teachers are thrown into the school and classroom to sink or swim. It's Darwinism in education, where only the strong survive. Except that "strong" doesn't always mean the teachers or leaders with the best skills. Sometimes the ones "selected" by the environment are simply those who can put up with a lot, or those who have limited options for gainful employment. They are suffering, the schools are suffering, and our children are suffering.

Teachers and leaders who enter public education without the prerequisite skills for teaching and leading pose great challenges to districts, as precious human resources that might be focused on deepening pedagogy and leadership must too often remain focused on developing even the most fundamental skills. Unfortunately, many districts don't have the resources or infrastructure to meet the needs of so many unprepared teachers and leaders through their talent-development programs. And because very little of the science of human performance is taught to district and school leaders, performance evaluations intended to motivate and help actually hurt and deepen the problem. Essentially, good people pursuing teaching and leadership are being thrown into a bad system. As the renowned management expert W. Edwards Deming noted, "A bad system will beat a good person every time." Focus must be taken off individual performance and placed on improving the system.

Now, we don't want to play the very blame game we frown on. It isn't our intention to point the finger at universities and other preparation programs. It is our wish that accrediting bodies and those advocating for improvement of teacher- and leadership-preparation programs implement the following:

- Place progressively greater focus on performance measures in order to recognize and reinforce programs that have been effective
- Completed a comprehensive analysis to discover the key components related to the success of effective preparation programs
- Support unsuccessful preparation programs with embedding these key components into their curriculum and instruction

The goal should be to increase the number of successful teacher- and leadership-preparation programs so that all teachers and leaders are adequately prepared to meet the needs of our children, and our children are prepared to meet the demands of a global society.

The good news is that it's starting to happen. A call to action is increasingly being made by various researchers and committees to improve teacher and leadership programs (e.g., the Wallace Foundation and the Wing Institute). Moreover, thought leaders across fields continue to clamor for changes in not only how we teach, but also what we teach and how we motivate students.

Dr. Joe Harless, a noted behavior scientist and advocate for evidence-based educational reform, called for a radical change in our country's approach to education in his book *The Eden Conspiracy* (2016). In it, he advocates for a bottom-up approach that determines the purpose and goals of education and works backward from there. An expert in performance engineering, he outlined this progression with examples for illustration.

Figure 3.2.

Harless's hard work may have not gone unheard, as legislation is popping up that attempts to align the needs of the workforce with the inputs provided by state education and universities. At the state level at this writing, forward-thinking legislators like those in Ohio are trying to pass House Bill 512 to merge the state education, higher education, and workforce departments into one. Proponents of the bill cite the large number of graduates who require remedial classes upon graduation as a need for the overhaul. Though met with opposition by the state school board, the purported goal of House Bill 512 is to have better alignment between these systems so that graduates are equipped with skills that better match those sought by colleges and employers.

And at the federal level, the Department of Education has announced regulations that require states to report on and rate teacher-preparation programs using a number of measures, including:

- student learning outcomes
- placement and retention rates
- feedback from graduates on the program
- feedback from employers on the program

While these regulations have been met with the ire from higher education, the robust conversations they've generated are important to all stakeholders. As our world continues to change, so do the learning needs of our students. As such, the need for teaching practices to keep evolving is logical. We must continue to design and realign preparation programs with the needs of students and schools if we are to allow them to meet the demands of global competitiveness.

And then we must ensure that required knowledge and skills be effectively transferred to new *and existing* teachers and leaders. This can be done by regularly reviewing and establishing objectives, analyzing tasks, identifying the most important standards, assessing teachers' and leaders' current repertoire, providing training in critical skills, and then *deliberately* coaching based on their needs.

Where Do We Go?

So why is this important and what does it have to do with this book? You've come to read it because you are a leader, coach, consultant, or stakeholder invested in supporting teacher success. The problem with some folks who support teachers is that they tend to end up playing the blame game too. And if you understand what's at the root of performance deficits, you might be more understanding and supportive. For decades, focus has been placed on telling teachers what they should be doing and providing poor evaluations when they don't do it.

If we want students to achieve, we must improve our methods of training and coaching teachers. Instead of telling, we must focus on helping. Even now, as teachers enter the workforce without adequate preparation, we must fight to support them. And leaders too! One of the advantages of this book is that the coaching process we outline can be used at any level within the school system. Whether we're talking about district leaders supporting school leaders or school leaders and coaches supporting classroom leaders, *Deliberate Coaching* can enable people to reach the highest levels of success through a measurable process that progressively helps educators perform a little bit better tomorrow than they did today.

CHAPTER 4

USE THE WHEEL, DON'T REINVENT IT!

Make things as simple as possible, but no simpler.

—Albert Einstein

When it's time for a new set of tires, a driver doesn't attempt to design a new tire. She goes to the local tire store, peruses the assortment of tires, and chooses the best tire for her car in her budget. While all of these tires are made by different brands, they all consist of the same basic combinations of materials that make up a tread and a body. These materials are developed and tested by scientists and regulated by agencies like the United States Department of Transportation. No person in their right mind would try a "flavor of the month" tire developed by the plumber around the corner as they set off on a cross-country trip. That would be silly and dangerous.

And yet, this "flavor of the month" approach has existed in education for decades. It is silly. And it is dangerous. It's also unnecessary, as a heavily researched process has already led to positive and sustainable outcomes across many areas. These areas include, but are not limited to:

- Animal training
- Autism spectrum disorder
- Behavioral medicine and health
- Organizational cultural change
- Economics
- Forensics
- Gambling
- Gerontology
- Marketing
- Mental health disorders
- Safety
- Parenting
- Physical health
- Schools and classrooms
- Sports

How can one process result in positive impacts across so many fields? In one word, science. Specifically, the science of human behavior. Like the engineering science that led to the development of tires that allow us to safely move from point A to point B, the science of human behavior has led to the development of processes that help people move toward meaningful outcomes.

You might be thinking, "What the heck does science have to do with coaching in education?" Well, as you likely now understand, science is *exactly* what education needs if we are going to make sustainable change. Science has literally changed our world and the way we interact with it. It's improved medicine, communication, access to knowledge, and travel, just to name a few examples.

And science is poised to tackle many other issues that ail the human condition. Issues related to crime, poverty, education, and more can all be tackled by science. But not just any science—applied behavior analysis, the science of human behavior whose purpose is improving socially significant behaviors and enhancing well-being. During its existence over the last half-century, ABA has helped improve lives through careful analysis and intervention. It has also informed policy, programs, and interventions of groups and organizations. And it can help solve complex global issues as well (Ledoux, 2014). This makes sense given that every person in the world can produce better outcomes through technology rooted in ABA. This includes educators and the systems that support them.

Behavior = Results

In a system as large and complex as education, it's easy to get caught up in the myriad of problems and look for the quick flavor-of-the-month fix. The politicians say, "Do this," the economists say, "Do that," and still countless other professionals tell educators, "Do the other." Then the high-paid consultant declares, "You have to do one more thing." And what's crazy is that most of them don't seem to care what professionals within the field of education think. It's enough to make your head spin.

Well, here's the good news. In a sense, they're all recommending the same thing: that something be "done." And at the basest level, they're correct. You see, all results require somebody doing something more, doing something less, or doing something differently. To put it simply, all results require behavior. The common variable amongst all the recommendations is that they involve people behaving. In education, different behaviors by different people lead to different results. For example, teachers instruct (this is behavior) in ways that lead to student learning (learning outcomes are a measure of behavior). Principals lead (leading is behavior) in a way that affects a school culture (culture is shared behavior). So it stands to reason that if we want to achieve desired results in education, we must first understand the principles of behavior, then identify the right behaviors that will get results in the right way.

We'll talk more about identifying the right behaviors later on. But first, let's take a minute to talk about right and wrong. When we say "right," we mean behaviors that are ethical and lead to positive outcomes. There are many examples of results being obtained the wrong way in education. One need only google "cheating on standardized tests" for a long list. From students and teachers to school and even district leaders, these folks sought to achieve the right results via the wrong behavior. This is why it's critical that focus be taken off outcomes like standardized-test scores and placed on the behavior required to achieve intended results.

In the best organizations, these behaviors are strategically aligned to obtain results quickly and efficiently. For example, at the district level, good superintendents collaborate with principals and district leaders to share their vision, identify goals, and identify leadership behaviors that are valued and required to reach those goals. At the school level, good principals collaborate with leadership teams to identify specific goals aligned with the school's vision and district goals, then embed the required behaviors of targeted staff into school improvement plans to see that these goals are accomplished. These principals specify the behaviors they value, then seek to support their leadership team with modeling behaviors that are consistent with these values.

At the classroom level, teachers collectively understand the vision and the behaviors that will lead to its realization. Their approaches to meeting the needs of the students are aligned with the values of the principal and reflect school improvement behaviors and goals outlined in the school improvement plan. Like a well-prepared football team that wins the Super Bowl, this strategic alignment allows schools to accelerate achievement by multiplying key behaviors that lead to established goals.

Oh, and this doesn't exclude you! Your behavior is a critical part of this puzzle. If you know what a teacher should be doing more of, less of, or differently to improve an outcome (like student achievement), then you must also understand what you have to do (how you should behave) to have a positive impact on the teacher's performance.

Fortunately, behavior analysts have stockpiled mountains of literature aimed at just that. It will show you how to arrange the environment (you are a part of a teacher's environment) in a way that brings out the best in people. Understanding why certain behaviors occur under certain circumstances and other behaviors don't will provide you with important knowledge for influencing those you support to choose more of the right behaviors under the right conditions.

Revisiting NCLB

We don't want to harp on this, but we're certain that our educational system would be far more successful had legislators understood basic behavioral principles. Remember all that talk about metacontingencies in chapter 1? Well, it still comes down to people at different levels doing something more, less, or differently. Making change at the systems level requires interlocking (think dependent on one another) behavior of people to produce aggregate outcomes that can't be achieved by any one individual (Glenn, 1991).

Here are some basic behavioral principles legislators clearly didn't understand when they enacted an educational reform law that affected the entire nation. You'll learn all about these critical elements of individual and organizational behavior change in the next section of our book, but for now, these will give you a little taste of concepts to come:

Establishing metrics. Before a school can get to where it wants to go, it must know where it is. Establishing an average baseline for an entire system doesn't take into account how each school is performing, or how each individual is performing. And when we say metrics, we're talking about data, measurement, or any sources of information that can be used to assess, correct, or reinforce performance improvement. Measurement is your best friend when you're trying to achieve a result. You may have a destination, but if you don't know where you are, or you don't know the direction you're going, you may never get there.

Goal setting. By setting a goal that 100 percent of students would be proficient by 2014, legislators didn't take into account the current performance of students or the capacity of those charged with helping students become proficient. Goal setting requires an understanding of goals and specific pinpointed behaviors and results, which we will detail in section 3.

Pinpointing. Pinpointing involves identifying specific and measurable behavior (pinpointed behavior) linked to specific and measurable desired results (pinpointed results) and understanding how these behaviors interact with one another at the individual, group, and organizational levels.

Shaping. The path to accelerating performance and improving achievement lies in the reinforcement of incremental and successful steps toward goals.

Feedback. Feedback is information, targeted at improving performance, about what a person is doing. All learning requires feedback. Feedback that is inconsistent or too far removed from performance has little to no positive impact on performance. In fact, lack of feedback frequently has a negative impact on performance and outcomes.

Motivation. Motivation is defined as a fundamental understanding of outcomes (consequences) and how they affect the future occurrence of behavior.

Before determining how to use these concepts to right the ship and set sail, you must first understand why it's sinking. Fortunately, organizational behavior management (OBM), a subfield of ABA with focus on making a positive difference in the workplace, has practical tools to help diagnose the problem. We will review this more throughout the book, but in the meantime think about it as a root cause analysis that determines the factors leading to both productive and nonproductive performance. Once completed, you can implement multilevel solutions for behavior, process, and system improvement to make a positive and sustainable impact on achievement (Sasson, Alvero, & Austin, 2006).

To improve performance in education, some of the key questions that can be answered when looking for your leadership solutions include the following: What are the desired results at each level of the organization, and what activities must each individual engage in to obtain these results? What variables most strongly influence performance at each level within the school system? What variables (e.g., policy, resources, training, and management) might be affecting performance in schools? What changes can we make to increase the performance to desired results? Discovering orderly relations between performance and the system in which it occurs provides the opportunity for meaningful improvement in the critical behaviors that ultimately lead to student achievement.

If we could only go back to a time before No Child Left Behind to gain an audience with lawmakers, we could guide these well-meaning folks toward developing a system that fosters behavior, routine, and habit change to positively impact student achievement. In a sense, we might be thankful for NCLB, as the failed effort has created opportunity for real change. Change that is purposeful, precise, and systematic. Change rooted in the application of OBM.

So we strongly encourage you to use the wheel and not reinvent it. A lot of good science has been conducted and applied over a long period of time to help us make good use of our time as educators and leaders. We don't have to rely on trial and error. We don't have to waste half a school year with approaches that don't work. This book offers a summary of some key areas of behavior analysis that we feel can benefit your leadership and culture and offers a few tools based on this science. We hope that this knowledge will help save you some time so that you can truly maximize the time you spend with your students.

SECTION 2

THE SCIENCE OF BEHAVIOR

CHAPTER 5

THE SCIENCE OF BEHAVIOR

Science is a way of thinking much more than it is a body of knowledge.

—Carl Sagan

Every school has its own distinctive culture. Your culture might be strong, boosting teachers' morale and enabling students to be happy and productive. Or your culture might be a liability, bogged down by barriers and obstacles that hinder performance. The good news is that culture isn't static; it can be improved. Your school's culture is made up of patterns of behavior—behavior of the students, teachers, administrators, and parents who make your school unique. And there's a logic behind this behavior.

For decades, behavior analysis has offered scientific support for building and sustaining behavior. This science of behavior provides the guidance and foundation that schools, businesses, communities, and any other place you can think of need to create the type of culture people are proud to be a part of. Why reinvent the wheel when you can learn from what exists and build on it? By doing so, you can avoid some of the costly educational pitfalls we've all faced at one time or another, many of which are highlighted in this book.

The ABCs of School Leadership

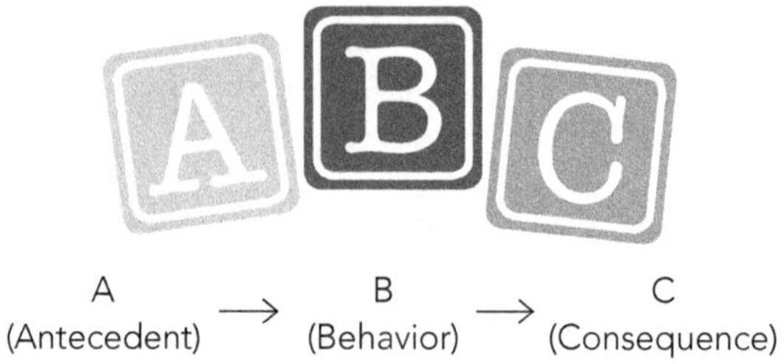

Figure 5.1.

Effective, efficient teacher behaviors lay the groundwork for sustainable student outcomes. These behaviors must be built—one way or another. Exemplar behaviors might occur naturally over long periods of time as a result of trial and error, or they might be trained systematically with a certain level of direction and precision. The purpose of any leadership system is to make it possible to build these behaviors in a way that minimizes the use of school resources and maximizes the impact of school leadership. To do this, we start at the beginning: with our ABCs.

Every job in an organization has specific behaviors that are critical to its success. A die setter in an injection molding plant must know how to run an injection press, a nurse at a hospital must know how to administer medications, and a teacher must know how to instruct. In order for these behaviors to occur, people receive training, review school procedures, and follow checklists. These *antecedents* (e.g., training, procedures, checklists) are things that come before a behavior and serve to get it started or prompt it to occur. However, whether people will continue to perform on the job is dependent on what happens *after* the behavior. If something desired follows a certain behavior, then this behavior will continue. If something undesired follows the behavior, then the behavior will go away. These are the *consequences* that determine whether a newly trained behavior will continue or will dissipate over time. All behavior, in and outside of the workplace, follows this *a*ntecedent-*b*ehavior-*c*onsequence sequence, or ABCs. This includes the behavior of our students, teachers, and school leaders. Let's take a deeper look at these ABCs.

Do you want your teachers to be good because of you or in spite of you?

You Gotta Find It First

The first step in helping a teacher be successful is to figure out what the desired teaching behaviors are. For instance, what are the student outcomes each teacher is responsible for, and what is the best path to get to those outcomes? You can't assume that a new teacher comes in with these best practices simply because they have a college degree, nor can you assume that teachers who get good student outcomes necessarily know exactly what they're doing to get those outcomes. It's common to hear things like "I just understand the students," "I like to empower the students," or "I just have a good group of students," none of which should give you confidence that they know what's working and what isn't. This leaves teachers identifying themselves as people with "good personalities," "passion," "charisma," and other vague descriptors of behavior hoping they'll continue to capture lightning in a bottle and the rest of us wishing that we had a different "personality." But it's not about personality. People aren't born good teachers. Good teaching behaviors like responding frequently and positively to students are built over time because certain things work, and certain things don't. Good school leaders find out what these behaviors are and then share this information in the form of antecedents (that is, training).

Start It Up

Once you have identified the outcomes of good teaching and the behaviors teachers should engage in to get to those outcomes, the next step is to make sure they can actually demonstrate these best practices. As we stated, antecedents come before behavior and serve to get it going. You provide teachers with instructions so they know the procedure. You provide them with training to build new skills to add to their repertoire, making them more capable of producing successful students in the classroom. You send people reminders about what to do and when to do it. The science tells us that behavior occurs because something prompts it to occur, whether we're aware of what that is or not. School leaders can set teachers up for success by building in these antecedents, maximizing the use of the staff and resources to guarantee that the right teaching is occurring in and out of the classroom.

An important consideration when using antecedents, however, is not to rely *too* much on them. Antecedents can be a fast way to check the box that you've addressed some sort of leadership need in your school. Teachers appear to be struggling with an area, so you fix a policy, provide training, or send out a memo, then move on. But this is just part of the equation. If all you do is get behavior started—the teachers demonstrate best practices in training, and they're starting to apply them in the learning environments—it will be likely to eventually cease if you stop there. So what's the next step?

"There Will Be Consequences"

Consequences determine if behavior will continue. Although the word "consequence" might leave a bad taste in your mouth, fear not. Consequences can be good or bad. They can be delivered by someone (e.g., praise, criticism) or occur naturally in the environment (e.g., try something new and save time, giving a ton of effort on a new task). Perhaps the consequence that keeps a teacher going is the success of a student on a test or perhaps it's recognition by a parent on out-of-classroom accomplishments; it's all dependent on the individual.

If something follows a behavior and the behavior increases, this means the person finds some sort of value in that consequence. We call this positive reinforcement. A teacher who likes it when students get a correct answer will engage in whatever behaviors result in students getting correct answers. A teacher who likes to receive praise from the principal will engage in whatever behaviors have led to praise in the past. If that reinforcement stops, then the behavior goes away. This is called *extinction*. In other words, much like dinosaurs disappeared or became *extinct* because there wasn't an environment to sustain them, behavior will eventually disappear too without a supportive or reinforcing environment.

If something is removed or avoided following a behavior and the behavior increases, we call this negative reinforcement. If a teacher finds that a classroom activity is time-consuming and difficult, she might avoid that activity. If a teacher does not want to be around the principal, she will do whatever is takes to avoid the principal.

Behavior maintained by negative reinforcement can also be extinguished if the person is no longer able to avoid or escape the bad outcome. For example, a teacher who doesn't like cleaning up before he leaves might ask an aide to stay late and clean. The aide cleaning up for him negatively reinforces (i.e., increases the likelihood the teacher will leave early) leaving before all of his duties are done. Once the aide stops doing that, the teacher will be forced to stay and clean himself.

The distinction between positive and negative reinforcement is important when you think about the type of coach you are and the type of coach you want to be. Do you only show up when something is wrong? If so, consider the effect this pattern of behavior has on your school culture. If something good happens in the classroom, nobody knows about it and the teacher is ignored. If something bad happens, a school administrator shows up. With these as the sole consequences, it's easy to see why some teachers will do just enough to avoid an uncomfortable situation—the uncomfortable situation being an encounter with you! Do you want your teachers to be good *because* of you or *in spite* of you?

Most teachers chose their career path because they genuinely care about children. They want to see their students succeed. The right teaching behaviors should lead to the right student outcomes. However, student outcomes aren't the only consequence of teaching. Teaching is hard. It takes effort. Doing it the right way can be time-consuming, and it's often a thankless job, with teachers only hearing from parents and administrators when something goes wrong. As a school leader, you can help by adding positive consequences—making good things happen more often for the right behaviors. There's a lot you can do by yourself in the form of praise, feedback, and other tenets of a good coaching system. And if a certain teacher has performance problems, you need to be sensitive to all the antecedents and consequences that surround this teacher's day-to-day performance.

In the case of a performance deficit, you can build better behaviors through the process of *shaping*. To shape, you simply identify the overall goal you want the teacher to achieve, figure out what the teacher is doing now, and reinforce incremental improvements toward that goal. For example, if you want a new preschool teacher to have the type of jovial, energetic interactions most seasoned teachers have with their students, you have to start where the teacher currently is. If the new teacher barely smiles and only communicates with a few of the children, you can't expect her to jump to your standards overnight. And if you simply choose to wait for her to do it, maybe providing more training because you assume she doesn't know how, you'll be waiting a long time. So you start small. Reinforce her simply talking more to the kids. Once she's doing that, start focusing your reinforcement on *how* she talks to the kids. Is she smiling? Is she laughing? Is she engaging the students with questions and pretend play? Slowly move toward the goal and reinforce her improvements along the way. This is the path to success for a good coach, and this is the way to maximize staff performance while building a positive school culture.

The teaching behaviors that have the strongest antecedents and the strongest consequences win. This means that if there are powerful antecedents pushing poor teaching and powerful consequences keeping those behaviors going, best practices will lose out to these less desirable methods. It's not necessarily because the teacher *can't* teach the right way or doesn't *want* to teach the right way. The school leader's job is to find out what's causing optimal and suboptimal teaching, make sure teachers have the skills, and use antecedents and consequences to refine and maintain those behaviors—show them that teaching the right way pays off for everyone.

The Ethics of Coaching

School leaders and all those charged with supporting teacher performance have likely been extensively trained in their craft. You probably had a very successful career as a teacher, with a proven track record of getting results, prior to taking responsibility for the performance of instructors who work to maintain the high standards you once set. The scope of your day-to-day work has drastically expanded—you've moved from classroom and student-based activities to administration and staff-management. Now you must lead your teachers in a way that generates the teacher performance that yields the best outcomes for the classroom and the school as a whole.

Although *ethics* is a broad concept, the central premise is this: getting results the right way. What is the right way in this case? Consistently supporting teachers rather than waiting for something to go wrong and popping in to let them know about it. Helping teachers rather than simply evaluating them. Building behaviors through positive reinforcement rather than relying solely on punitive measures for performance problems. And, perhaps most importantly, focusing not just on school and classroom results, but how those results are attained.

An initial responsibility of new leaders, regardless of industry, is to identify their new responsibilities and assess their own strengths and weaknesses. However, even if you have no prior training or supervised experience leading others, the basic principles (ABCs) of behavior that were responsible for your success as a teacher still apply; they just need to be redirected toward building a workforce for high-performing teachers instead of a classroom of high-performing students. Positive reinforcement can accelerate teacher performance just as it did for your students when you used it in the classroom. You just need to be able to take a bird's-eye view of your role and see how you can expand your understanding of learning and performance to a group with vastly different needs.

Just as teachers have ethics and conduct codes, so does the field of behavior analysis. Ethics codes help guide folks on how to work within a particular industry, using that industry's tools, in a respectful and responsible way. The science of behavior offers powerful tools that help to understand and improve all facets of performance. To guide this practice, the Behavior Analyst Certification Board (BACB) has a *Professional and Ethical Compliance Code* that all behavior analysts credentialed by the board must follow. As coaches start to apply the science of behavior to their respective coaching practices, it's important to consider some key areas of ethical practice.

Set the Teacher Up for Success

Coaches should consider any environmental conditions and other barriers that might be interfering with teacher performance. This helps set teachers up for success and frees them to engage in the kind of optimal performance they're capable of. There are a number of items that could hinder an otherwise high-performing teacher. Perhaps the teacher is capable of exemplary performance but simply hasn't been trained (can't demonstrate the skills you're looking for when asked). The teacher's lack of skills is a barrier that you need to address. Environmental conditions such as a lack of materials, large class sizes, and procedural or scheduling problems can interfere with performance as well. Perhaps a group activity is designed to take thirty minutes to complete, but a teacher is consistently left with only fifteen minutes. This suggests that you need to help the teacher figure out why her schedule is consistently off and how to fix it. Perhaps another activity is taking too much time.. Maybe the activity is taking too long because of student disruptions that need to be addressed. Whatever the issue, it's the job of a good leader to identify the barriers to success.

It's Not Just about Poor Performance

Coaches are ultimately responsible for getting more good performance, not just less poor performance. If you just focus on stopping poor performance, you'll have a workforce searching for what to do instead. Consider the following example. Mountain High has a teacher-management program that consists of large lectures in the auditorium during professional-development days, teacher evaluations conducted twice during the year, write-ups for teacher performance problems, and a tenure system. The professional-development days involve the teachers gathering to listen to a speaker a few times a year. There are no demonstrations of learning or structured opportunities to engage during the training; it's simply a presentation. While this means that the impact is unknown, trainings like this aren't likely to build more than a general awareness of the content. The teacher evaluations are designed to check in on the teachers, and the measures include subjective items like "Instructor is creative in their approach." and "Instructor is efficient." But this feedback is delivered infrequently, it usually doesn't come until long after the behaviors have occurred, and it's too subjective to have an effect. Write-ups for teacher infractions like tardiness or other rule violations rely on punishment to decrease behavior; while this isn't necessarily a bad thing, they don't positively reinforce desired behaviors (e.g., showing up on time, following school rules). In addition, overreliance on punishment is likely to have a detrimental impact on your culture as it sometimes elicits strong emotional responses from those being punished that can have a negative ripple effect across the school. Finally, while the tenure system provides job security, it doesn't recognize teacher performance.

Overall, Mountain High's system involves infrequent contact with teachers, thus limited support for them, and relies on ineffective evaluation procedures and more punitive measures which can often lead to an adverse climate and increased rates of teacher attrition. Least-restrictive alternatives mean that you start with procedures to support the teachers before resorting to more punitive measures. You can't achieve your goals as a leader simply by focusing on decreasing behavior. Results come by people doing the right things, and these things occur through your use of antecedents (e.g., training, prompts) and reinforcement.

Feedback

We talk a lot about feedback in this book and for good reason: it's essential and it works! Coaches need to provide timely feedback to supervisees and use reinforcement systems that improve their performance. The Deliberate Coaching system is designed to offer an avenue for this feedback. You can't provide feedback unless you know the specific behavior you're targeting from the teacher and why that behavior is important. The feedback conversation needs to include this information so the teacher understands. If not, this isn't likely to have an impact on performance—it's simply a conversation, not a feedback conversation. Feedback should be paired with something of value to the teacher, such as praise or showing them how the performance described in the feedback fixes a personal concern they're having in their day-to-day work (natural reinforcers such as saving time or seeing the progress in your students). These natural reinforcers can be very powerful as they do not require someone else to deliver them, thus they often occur more immediately and more frequently than those reinforcers that coaches deliver. This helps feedback to function as a reinforcer and actually improve performance. Constructive feedback that identifies poor performance and includes a discussion of the replacement behavior needs to be followed up with an opportunity to positively reinforce that replacement behavior. If it doesn't, the teacher might go through all the effort of doing the new behavior without seeing the benefit of that behavior. Feedback isn't necessarily reinforcement, but it can be. Consistent feedback can have a significant impact on performance, and it's critical for all leaders.

Again, these principles are generalizable to any area of leadership. The principles of behavior analysis are in effect whether you're addressing a student's behavior, a teacher's behavior, or a coach's behavior. If behavior is occurring, it's occurring because of positive reinforcement or negative reinforcement (e.g., avoidance). If behavior is not occurring, it's because there are more contingencies of punishment keeping the behavior down than reinforcers keeping it going. As a result, behavior analysis is applicable to any person responsible for behavior change—including school leaders. Ethical coaching means focusing not just on the outcomes, but how you get those outcomes. You don't want teachers doing the bare minimum to get by, and you don't want a culture where people do whatever it takes to get results, no matter how questionable those practices might be. If you're a teacher, psychologist, counselor, or other kind of school professional, you might have your own ethics code that you abide by, and we strongly encourage you to continue to do so. These professional and ethical standards are put in place to protect you and those you work with. Our hope is that their similarity to the ethics of behavior analysis will lead to a continuously developing ethical repertoire that you and your colleagues will value.

Building Habits

We've talked a bit about natural reinforcement, but its importance to the long-term success of a coaching system cannot be overstated.

Learning to play an instrument can be a time-consuming, difficult, yet rewarding process. You might fool around on the piano and attempt to teach yourself, ready to see whether your inevitable talent will result in your being a jazz prodigy or more of a rockstar! After a few failed attempts at *Chopsticks* you'll either give it up or seek some lessons. But the lessons are no easy feat. There is a lot of study, a lot of time with instructors, and countless hours of flat notes and missed keys that drive you and your neighbors mad. Yet you continue. The instructor is taking it slow, providing encouragement for each new note combination and new section of a piece. Your family and friends are supportive, smiling and supporting you like you're playing a beautiful ballad. And you need that support at a high level early on.

Now fast-forward a bit. You've learned a piece or two. The compliments start to sound more genuine, and people actually seem to be enjoying your music! But you're also seeking those reinforcers less and playing more on your own. You're liking what you hear when you play, so you keep playing. You're building *habits*. You're playing music not because you have to, not because others are encouraging you—you're doing it because it's fun and you want to!

Habits are established when you access the natural reinforcers in your environment. Natural consequences occur all the time, and they're all around you. Some of them are good, like the reinforcing sound of music. Some are bad, like the amount of effort it took to get that music to sound good! One of the reasons natural consequences are so valuable, particularly natural reinforcers, is that they don't require anyone to deliver them. They are consistent and often occur immediately after the behavior. You hit the key on the piano and you hear the note. When that note is bad, it punishes your hitting that key. When that note is good, it reinforces your hitting that key. But if the only thing controlling your behavior is natural consequences when you're just starting out, the frequent, powerfully annoying sound of hitting the wrong keys will vastly overpower the infrequent sound of hitting the right keys. So why do you keep practicing? You keep practicing because you get a significant amount of external reinforcement that maintains this behavior while you're starting to access the natural reinforcers. This is the job of a coach—to make the connection between improvements in behavior and natural consequences.

Let's take this back to school. When you introduce a new concept to any workplace, it's typically going to involve a bit of a learning curve. Learning will take a lot of time and effort until the person gets comfortable. Say you want a teacher to increase student engagement during activities by asking more questions and providing more detailed feedback to students to prompt continued responses. Prior to your intervention, the teacher told you that lessons have been getting harder to run, students are acting out, and the test scores of the students in his classroom are low. But he has his own history of reinforcement, things that he's done for years because he feels they're working. If he didn't feel there was a reason to run his activities in a particular way, then he wouldn't be doing it. People do what they do because it works for them. Perhaps their behaviors aren't producing the optimal outcomes, but to them, it's working! This is what you're competing with when you introduce a new requirement.

Now you introduce your new method. The teacher understands and is ready to go. He tries to change his ways to match your expectations, but he's struggling and students are noticing. Lessons seem to be getting harder and more confusing and students are doing worse on the tests and are starting to get upset. So the coach provides feedback and increased support, pointing out that he's getting a lot of students responding, but he needs to tweak how he's providing feedback. After a while, he gets the hang of things and it's paying off. Students are performing better and his days are getting easier. After a while the coaching support moves toward other things the teacher is doing, checking back from time to time to reinforce the continued progress he's making with running those activities.

What happened in that classroom? At first, the natural consequences of high effort and poor results would have kept the teacher from doing what the coach asked if the coach and the principal didn't jump in for continued support. After a while, the new method started to work. And the coach made sure the teacher knew it. This demonstrated the value in the coaching relationship and showed that good things happen when he worked with his coach on improvements.

The goal of coaching is to build good workplace habits. Coaches do this by making the link between coaching suggestions and natural reinforcement. This is how you build exemplar teachers who can see the impact of their improvements. And this is how a coach can use the limited time they have to work on multiple behaviors during a school year. You can't do frequent and consistent coaching on the same behavior multiple times per week throughout the entire year. At some point you'll run out of time and you'll need to support the teacher on other things. But if you simply cut off the reinforcement you're providing *without* making that link to natural reinforcement, you're putting the behavior on extinction—decreasing performance because you've cut off the main source of reinforcement. Until other natural reinforcers can take over, such as seeing that progress saves time and actually works with their students, you need to keep providing external reinforcement like praise and positive feedback. Because this can't last forever, it's imperative that coaching conversations constantly help the coachee see the value in their day-to-day work.

Goal Setting

At some point in your coaching planning and conversations, you'll need to collaborate with the teacher to set some goals. Or, if you're a leader coaching one of the coaches, then you'll need to collaborate with them to set goals. Where you set these goals can have a big impact on performance. Consider the notion of a stretch goal, where you set the goal far out of reach. The idea is that people will work extra hard to achieve it, even though it might take superhuman effort.. But think about what you've learned about reinforcement and extinction. People do what they do because a positive reinforcer occurs as a result of that behavior. If someone is used to getting a reinforcer and that reinforcer stops, the behavior will decrease (move toward extinction). Consider your boss praising you for staying late for work. It takes a lot of time, but you appreciate that the boss notices and seems to care. If the boss stops this, then you might stop staying late because the reinforcement has stopped. If someone never accesses reinforcement in the first place, extinction won't occur (since there's no previous reinforcement to stop); the behavior simply won't get started (e.g., you wouldn't start staying late in the first place). So if the main reinforcer for a behavior is delivered upon reaching an unreachable goal, what type of impact do you think the stretch goal will have on behavior? Not much!

Goals need to be attainable. In fact, coaches should break up their goals. It could take a long time for a teacher to reach an ultimate performance goal and coaches can't just wait around to reinforce until the end. There is an experimental design in behavior analysis called a changing criterion design. The idea is that you first set a goal slightly above current performance, then raise it a bit more once you're hitting the first goal consistently, then raise it a bit more once you're hitting the second goal consistently, and so on. If reinforcement is delivered upon hitting those incremental goals, you have a high rate of reinforcement along the way to achieving your final goal. You do this instead of simply waiting until the individual hits an attainable yet faraway goal.

Say you're training for a marathon. The coach doesn't start by setting a goal for you to run twenty miles. The coach starts by saying that the goal for your long run in the first couple of weeks is five miles. After you hit that goal consistently you can move to seven. Once you're comfortable with seven, the goal moves to ten. You don't hit mile twenty until the end of your training, but your running is still being reinforced along the way for hitting these subgoals.

Now consider goals you might set for your teachers. Perhaps a teacher, in a given fifteen-minute activity, only gets responses from 5 percent of her students. You've tracked this for some time and it seems to be consistent. This is the teacher's baseline level of performance, where she's at without your intervening. Most teachers can get at least 80 percent of their students interacting during a fifteen-minute group activity. So do you start by setting the goal for that teacher at 80 percent? Probably not. Unless you've identified a pretty simple fix for why their rate is so low, most likely this change will take a bit of time. The teacher might need to change a few things she's doing. And remember, she's doing what she's currently doing for a reason. Something about it is working for her based on her current skill sets, even if it's not working for the students!

If it's not student engagement, it might be that the procedure is easy or the teacher just simply doesn't know what else to do. You have to find out what's going on and plan to build the alternative behaviors until you finally reach the goal. You know the rate at which you can increase the goal by tracking performance. If you want the teacher to provide all students a chance to respond during a given activity, but she is currently only getting to 20 percent of them, then start with a goal of 30 percent. Start small with the goal. Change can be hard, and you want to support the teacher by working with her to find ways to succeed and providing a lot of positive reinforcement, especially early on. Once you've identified the reason for the low performance and started to provide the support the teacher needs, maybe you start at 7 percent or 10 percent. Show the teacher that you notice the changes in performance, make sure she recognizes these changes, and ensure she knows these changes will be reinforced. There's nothing worse than spending a long time doing things a certain way, being asked to change, and getting ignored once you make the change. Setting subgoals helps provide a reinforcing path to success.

How you use reinforcement in conjunction with the goals you set will affect how well the goal works to improve performance. Sometimes, simply hitting the goal can function as a reinforcer. But remember that we say "*can* function" because you only know if something is actually a reinforcer when behavior increases after it occurs. One of the many benefits of tracking performance is that it gives coaches something objective to discuss with the teacher. "You're currently getting through about three lessons." That's a clear, reliable measure that you can get agreement on after your observation of a teacher. Next week when you observe, you can tell the teacher that he got through five lessons in the time he typically only gets through three. Sometimes just seeing the progress can help, especially when the teacher sees that you're acknowledging it.

But there are ways that you can raise how reinforcing it might be for someone to hit a particular goal. You want your coachees to care that they hit the goal, so there are things you can do to help with this. The process of pairing in behavior analysis means that you can take something that has limited to no reinforcing value and create a new reinforcer by consistently delivering both the proven reinforcer with the new reinforcer-to-be. For example, going on a walk might be extremely reinforcing to your dog. Before you go for a walk, you might reach for the leash. Eventually, after repeated pairings of the leash and the walk, simply grabbing the leash will cause your dog to go crazy. People work in the same way. Perhaps you've seen that praise from you, a respected supervisor, functions as a reinforcer. If you praise someone for a specific behavior, and that behavior increases after you deliver it, then praise from you is a reinforcer for this individual. (Note that this doesn't mean praise from everyone will function as a reinforcer.) In this case, you can deliver praise when the teacher hits a goal, and this will eventually make hitting the goal function as a reinforcer even without the accompanying praise. This pairing process is valuable when you're trying to identify and build reinforcers. You can pair goal setting with any type of reinforcer to raise the value of hitting that goal. If you're tracking performance on a graph or chart, you can also place a goal line on it as a form of graphic feedback. Then the person will see a representation of their performance in relation to the goal, which is another potential opportunity for reinforcement. In the same manner, you can pair *yourself* with reinforcement so then people are excited for you and your coaching!

Goal setting can help coaches incorporate all pinpointing, tracking, and reinforcement strategies into a valuable plan to help someone reach his or her potential. Coaches should set clear expectations of where current performance is and where people need to go. Use it wisely, as it's a valuable addition to your coaching toolbox.

CHAPTER 6

BUILDING TEACHER PERFORMANCE

When you're curious, you find lots of interesting things to do.

—Walt Disney

The importance of education, training, and professional development is most likely not lost on those who have dedicated their lives to educating others. Classroom and schoolwide results are driven by behavior, and these behaviors need to be developed. Students must be trained to meet the requirements of their curricula and their lives, teachers must be trained to teach the students, and coaches must be trained on how to coach the teachers. We've all been involved in training in one way or another.

Training can be a costly and time-consuming process, but scientific advancements can offer a path to take advantage of some of these innovative new solutions. Whether building performance online or through an on-site instructor, the exponential advancements in computer-based technology are enabling state-of-the-art learning environments that learners will both benefit from and gravitate toward. But computer-based technology is not the only area of scientific advancement that impacts training effectiveness. Behavioral science accelerates learning and makes it more efficient.

Many seasoned leaders will tell you that training and professional development can be one of the most frustrating and complex endeavors of any organization. Given the demands placed on leaders to evolve and produce results across different types of learners regardless of barriers in their environment, you can see how it might wear down even the most positive and energetic person. Whether you're an administrator, a new principal, a schoolteacher, or simply someone trying to learn a new hobby at home, training systems involve a number of critical pieces that must be respected in order to get to the ultimate critical goal: creating a skill that has demonstrable value.

Tackling these critical skills efficiently produces results, hopefully making life easier on both the leader and direct report. But *are* these critical pieces respected?

Those wishing to become college professors are trained diligently for years in graduate school to be experts in their field. Once these individuals graduate, they will be tasked with taking their vast knowledge of physics, mathematics, art, or whatever else they dedicated a lifetime of student loan payments to and teaching others to do what they do as educators. The problem? Just because you're an expert physicist doesn't mean you know how to teach people physics.

The issue isn't restricted to academia. Wayne Gretzky, who held over sixty National Hockey League records when he retired, had a winning percentage of under .500 as a coach. Isaiah Thomas, Ted Williams, Magic Johnson, and numerous other Hall of Fame athletes have shared a similar fate. Just because you're one of the greatest athletes in your sport doesn't mean that you know how to educate people in your sport. Just because you're good at math and science doesn't mean that you know how to educate people in math and science. And just because you were a good teacher doesn't mean that you know how to educate teachers.

Educating the Educators

The first step in an educator's education occurs when a person decides to become an educator. This journey can start from a number of places. Perhaps the individual comes from a family of educators and has always seen the value of helping others reach their potential. Maybe she was always really good with kids and saw teaching as a perfect avenue to inspire young people and build the next generation of enlightened and passionate citizens. Or maybe she had always been told that the way *she* explained something always made more sense. Teaching is a noble profession with endless demands and has been since the beginning of civilization. Once someone commits to becoming an educator, the next step is to—you guessed it—educate that person first.

But what do educators need to know? And how does that compare to what teachers receive during their college and post-college education? For example, if you look at the average curriculum for instructional design degrees, you'll see numerous classes on learning systems design, assessment, computer technology—even a few on learning theories. But odds are you won't see classes on *behavior analysis*, the science behind learning. Think about the classes you took as an educator. Were there more courses on subject content than on shaping behaviors associated with learning, getting students in touch with positive reinforcement, or perhaps other topics on the science behind dealing with behavior problems? You most likely had more content-oriented classes. That's unfortunate, as there's a science behind successfully building performance in and out of the classroom that goes beyond theory, beyond basics in subject matter and curriculum, and beyond relying too much on experience.

Using Science to Teach

Every teacher will have their own style, their own way to get students to engage, their own way to identify and use reinforcers. But there is a science to building student skills and managing classroom performance that should not be ignored. You wouldn't let teachers use trial and error to figure out which chemicals should be mixed together during chemistry class, would you? Similarly, you shouldn't require teachers to use trial and error to figure out how to build student skills and manage classroom performance.

Teachers set up their respective learning environments so students can practice. Some of the activities are individualized (e.g., completing a worksheet, answering a question) and some of them occur as part of a group (e.g., working on a group project, responding in unison to a question), but they should all be targeted toward practice. Practice makes perfect, right? Not quite. There is science behind what type of practice works. Ericsson, Krampe, and Tesch-Römer (1993) argued that practice must be "deliberate" to maximize performance, a claim that has been well researched over the years (de Bruin, Smits, Rikers, & Schmidt, 2008). Deliberate practice centers on repetition and feedback that's both positive and constructive. The science has told us that students need significant opportunities for learning and practice (e.g., Johnson & Layng, 1992, 1994). We will reflect on this important concept again later in the book as it relates to Deliberate Coaching.

Understanding why people do what they do can help build a classroom environment that uses science (behavior analysis) to maximize teaching effectiveness. As we've discussed, one of the basic tenets of behavioral science is that behavior occurs because antecedents prompt the behavior and reinforcement keeps it going. A child raises her hand to answer a question because, in the past, this has been reinforced by the teacher praising the student. Generally speaking, the more opportunities for children to engage in these activities, the faster they'll learn. Add a speed component to your accuracy standards, and these skills can be learned even faster and last longer in their repertoire. This is one of the core teaching practices illustrated in the Morningside Academy approach. A learner has two options once a skill is taught: use it or lose it. If the child uses the skill in day-to-day life or, at the very least, in subsequent lessons, then the child has continued opportunities to practice that skill and receive positive reinforcement for its use. If you teach a child to read a word, they have to keep practicing this skill when learning how to read sentences. If you teach a child to dribble a basketball, they have to keep practicing this skill when learning to play as part of a team. But if the child doesn't have the opportunity to practice these skills to fluency, they'll eventually go away. School curricula should be built to ensure that the skills kids learn are either built into their day-to-day lives (to access natural reinforcement) or built into subsequent curricula. For those skills that aren't, the best-case scenario is to teach them in a way that makes them last until an opportunity arises to use them again. For example, using flashcards with spelling, multiplication tables, and foreign languages increases the odds that these skills will stick even if the child doesn't use them all the time. This type of fluency training (utilizing speed plus accuracy) has been shown to result in faster, longer-lasting skill acquisition than traditional training that only focuses on how accurate people are during a learning activity (Bucklin, Dickinson, & Brethower, 2000; Fox & Ghezzi, 2003).

Classrooms should be built to maximize learning opportunities. If teachers did not receive sufficient education on the science of behavior in college, then school coaches can step in to help. We need to ensure that teachers have all the tools they need to be successful!

Onboarding the Educators

Even with the best college programs, it's not possible, nor should it be possible, to get all of the pertinent information, experience, and practice needed to be a successful educator in college. Continued education and professional development is an essential part of building teacher performance that lasts. Such continued education and development can be proactive, giving teachers new and refined skills to set them up for success. They can also be reactive, undertaken as a result of a performance deficit. The ABCs of behavior analysis are an essential part of this process.

To train critical teaching behaviors, the training itself contains antecedents to prompt behavior in the training environment and consequences to build these behaviors. The type of behaviors learners engage in during training will depend on the type of training system. Traditional instructor-led training might involve learners taking notes, answering questions aloud during large-group discussion, or participating in group or individual exercises. Antecedents such as textbooks, training handouts, or lecture slides presented by the instructor are often used to get people engaged during the training. Instructor feedback, peer praise, and grades are types of consequences that affect whether the behaviors being trained will continue and build. If we see more of these targeted learner behaviors as a result, then we say that *learning* has occurred.

Another form of training, computer-based instruction, offers a number of textual, auditory, and graphic displays as antecedents to prompt the types of behaviors possible on computer systems, such as typing a response, dragging and dropping options, and clicking to select an answer. The science of behavior shows us that what happens during or after these behaviors will determine how fast people will learn. These consequences include events that take place within the program, such as textual praise acknowledging a correct answer, and those that take place outside of the computer-training environment, such as praise from an instructor or successful application of something learned.

Each kind of training program offers a unique way to build behaviors, and each learner has their own unique history of learning and preferred way of learning. But the building blocks of learning—learning opportunities—are the same. A learning opportunity is the interaction of a training antecedent (e.g., an instructional statement), a learner responding to that antecedent, and a consequence following that response (e.g., feedback). Decades of research have shown that learning occurs when people capitalize on the quantity and quality of these learning opportunities (e.g., Binder, 1996). Yet we are all familiar with training programs that present hours of lecture-based antecedents before a learner finally has an opportunity to respond, only for the opportunity to be in the form of a quiz that allows you to "pass" with 80 percent accuracy. You can't expect competent teacher or leader performance to occur when the only feedback provided occurred one time, at the end of a long lecture in the form of some quiz. This is an error, a big one that wastes time and money with no return on investment. Taking advantage of the science of behavior behind learning and performance can help maximize the impact of your training systems and avoid costly training errors.

If It Ain't Broke, Don't Fix It

Regardless of the information spanning years of research on what works and what doesn't work regarding training practices, the standard professional-development day in schools often follows the same formula: pick a topic or two, get a speaker to lecture about the topics, and hope that it sticks. But we know that doesn't work. The science behind educating educators—and more importantly, the tips and tricks we've learned from that science—is often overlooked or ignored. And these trends are going to continue. Why is this?

Sometimes It Works

There are times when a trainer or a coach with no history of training or coaching can come out of nowhere and show you a unique skill set they happened to acquire during their previous work experience. You might just roll the dice and hope that this person does well, or you might have a strategic interviewing process that helps narrow things down. For example, if the person can describe the critical behaviors required of the job during the interview process, you'll have a certain level of confidence that they're not going to waste time with ineffective practices. You can compare the behaviors they cite with behaviors recommended in books like this one to make sure they meet your standards. If a person cannot describe these behaviors, then you're really just crossing your fingers and hoping for the best.

It Doesn't Work—But You Don't Know It

Sometimes the way we evaluate success fails to expose a real need for change. There are a number of ways to measure the success of training systems, some more applicable to learning than others.

- *Cost.* Just because your training was expensive doesn't mean that it taught anyone anything.
- *Test scores or activity completion.* Even if people passed a quiz or two or completed some activities, that doesn't mean they can apply those skills in the classroom at a high level.
- *Participant ratings.* People might rate your training highly, but you don't know whether they did so because the training was easy (and ineffective) or because it actually produced new skills.

Understanding your training metrics offers a level of precision that can really help guide how and when you train, but this can be easily missed or ignored. And if the science of behavior is not taught as part of instructional-design or professional-development seminars, you might not know what you've been missing.

There is a growing base of proven strategies that can help you assess and develop training systems. This book showcases those strategies and presents practical ways that you can add value to your training system. You will be provided with a toolbox you can use regardless of industry and regardless of training platform. Each time you reach into your science toolbox, you're helping prevent wasteful practices that can hurt your organization, your colleagues, and possibly even your career. By making a few slight adjustments here and there, you can capitalize on fast, efficient methods of developing training systems and post-training coaching systems that work and remain effective over time.

CHAPTER 7

MISUSE OF TRAINING

Most people spend more time and energy going around problems than in trying to solve them.

—Henry Ford

As the demand for training innovation increases, we can't leave behind the scientific foundation on which all learning is built. We can use this foundation to improve the way we educate the educators, building our training systems in a way that saves time and money without compromising quality and effectiveness. Combining technological advancements with the evidence-based training methods discovered through years of research on the science of behavior, there is a prime opportunity for companies to maximize the time spent on training and maximize long-term impact. This is what the science of behavior has to offer: a set of tips and resources you can use to ensure that your training expectations match your training development.

Training takes time, and time is money. A few errors here and there in the preparation and rollout of your training can waste resources and cause undue frustration. A subject-matter expert or senior teacher can give you a seemingly endless list of competencies that need to be addressed in a given teacher-education program. It's tempting to teach all of these, and it's even more tempting to try to teach them all at once. This is a mistake, and it can be a costly one.

Your training priorities influence your use of resources. How these resources are used directly affects the return on investment that your school administrators might be requesting. A clear understanding of training needs and optimal value provides an understanding of the specific behavior and results that will guide training efforts and set your training systems up for success. As a school leader trying to make the best use of time and resources, you should consider sifting through all the things that *can* be trained and narrowing them down to what *should* be trained. This leaves you with a set of behaviors that you're confident need to be trained; however, some of them will still be more critical than others. A trainer *can* spend professional development days teaching teachers and staff everything about the history of the school, advancements in school testing and why those occurred, different strategies they went through prior to deciding on implementing a Deliberate Coaching approach, etc., but there isn't time for that and it's not necessary for the teachers and staff to be successful. If you can't narrow the focus of your training to just those critical things that people need to thrive, then you're almost certainly setting yourself up for retraining. And if your training isn't effective in the first place, simply doing it over and over again won't magically make it work.

Every staff member in every school needs antecedents like training to prompt workplace behaviors and consequences like positive reinforcement and feedback to keep those behaviors going. Coaches should make sure that the right antecedents and consequences are being used so the behaviors you want prevail and those you don't want decline. Nonetheless, performance problems will persist. There will be things going on that shouldn't be, like a teacher failing to develop rapport with students, setting low student expectations, engaging in inappropriate peer-to-peer gossip, or cutting corners. Or there might be behaviors you want, but they don't occur enough, aren't occurring at a high enough level, or aren't occurring at all. For example, say you want teachers to ask questions of their students. It becomes a problem if they're questioning the same students over and over again while ignoring the struggling students who are too afraid or unsure of their answers to immediately raise their hands.

So, again, the question becomes *why* are these problems occurring. Training is time-consuming and can be costly, and it's a waste of resources to apply it to a non-training problem

The Quick Fix

Consider this example:

A few years back, a school district hired a consultant to assist with their staff-management programs. Part of their request was that the consultant guide the development of systems being integrated into a new school program designed to support children diagnosed with autism spectrum disorders. But prior to the consultant's involvement, there was an incident in gym class involving a disruptive child. The child was acting out, bothering the gym teacher and other students, and the situation escalated to the point where the gym teacher struck the child. The school requested training—specifically, training for all staff on general information about autism spectrum disorders and the ramifications of striking any child.

Do you think the teacher believed that hitting a child was the right thing to do? Do you think a lack of understanding about autism caused the teacher to do something she knew was wrong? More importantly, do you think the proposed training would fix the problem and prevent further incidents like this one?

Therein lies the issue. We don't know. We can't know without asking the right questions, without assessing or at least having a reliable guess as to what caused the problem. Reliance on assumption, personal experience, and common sense can impede effective decision-making and will, more often than not, lead to errors.

The training systems in our schools make up just one of the many tools leaders have in their toolbox to help address performance problems. Training doesn't fix all performance problems, even if your professional-development colleagues are consistently your first call whenever people make mistakes. The best leaders aren't just effective, they're also efficient. They know *why* a solution should be used . . . including training.

So why do we typically use training? The answer to this might seem obvious. Maybe all of the people receiving it are new teachers, looking to complete their required onboarding process. It's impossible for each new teacher to start the first day of employment with a repertoire that's already filled with your critical school information. Maybe your school got new state-of-the-art technology that everyone needs to get up to speed with. The only way the technology will work is if people are taught how to use it, so training is a given. Or maybe there are slated professional-development days, and training is what you do during these days. But let's not forget the fundamental purpose of training: to build skills not yet in an individual's repertoire or refine skills in a way that produces maximum impact. When looking to achieve this goal in an efficient and effective manner, you can't only take into account how *well* training is delivered; what's driving the *demand* for training is equally critical. Training should be used to address a need for training. It shouldn't be a one-size-fits-all bandage for all performance problems. Understanding this is the best way to position you and your training services for success.

Using Training to Punish

Training is fundamentally designed to build a skill set and prompt behavior. Even with this underlying premise, however, it often has a dual purpose. When used as a management tool, training might be delivered *after* performance, particularly poor performance.

As you now know, the science of behavior shows us that antecedents come before behavior to get it going and consequences come during or after behavior to increase, maintain, or decrease it. A principal might notice that a teacher is failing to chart student progress and assume that this is because the teacher doesn't understand how to do it. And sometimes the principal might not even question if the teacher knows how to do it. They simply might just feel it's necessary to punish the poor performance and send a "message" to the teacher and others by requiring them to attend training. Regardless of intent, training in this context is being used as a consequence, delivered as a result of behavior. It's a punishment for the undesired behavior that preceded the training (teaching without charting student progress) in addition to being an antecedent for the desired behaviors targeted during the training (charting progress).

It's possible to use training to both build and to correct, as a proactive skill builder and a reactive performance-management solution. However, if you use it improperly, you could inadvertently decrease existing behaviors that are effective instead of addressing the real cause of the performance problem. Moreover, if it's deliberately used as a punishment, the message you send may actually hamper performance of the teacher, or even negatively impact the performance of other teachers as the result of the negative ripple effect that punishment can sometimes have on climate and culture.

Retraining for the Sake of Retraining

We've established that training applied as a reactive performance-management solution is training applied in a dual role. If employed properly, this kind of training will target performance deficits. You teach someone because they have something they need to learn. This means that, based on either assessment or assumption, low or poor performance has resulted in a need for a solution and you've identified training as the way to fix it. Training follows behavior as a consequence and is then used as an antecedent to build or refine the right behaviors.

Reliance on assumption … can impede effective decision-making and will, more often than not, lead to errors.

At first glance, this seems to make sense. As part of its dual role, training is designed to get behavior going and, in the case of poor performance, get the desired behaviors going (e.g., effective instruction). But there is a subtle yet significant problem here. You're assuming that training will fix the problem, that a lack of training *was* the problem. But what if that assumption is wrong? Are the performance deficits truly caused by a lack of knowledge and skills needed to do the job. Always assuming that someone's performance problems occur because they lack a skill set can be demoralizing for the individual.

We can attest that, regardless of industry and performance issue, training and retraining will be at the forefront in most discussions on performance-improvement solutions. You yourself can most likely produce a series of examples. Maybe school leadership has been told that poor performance persists because there's something the professional-development content missed. An administrator might propose that poor performance will be fixed if the teacher can only receive more training and see it modeled. Perhaps the teacher has been told that performance problems will go away if the teacher's assistants can only be trained on how important these duties are to the school. These misconceptions occur because we can't truly explain why we are training; we can't explain what caused the performance problem. Given the time, effort, and resources needed for training, this can be a costly error that leaves you with the same performance problems you started with.

Jack of All Trades, Master of None

Even though training systems are ultimately designed to meet a performance need, there is no denying that there can be administrative pressures to get training done and get it done quickly. It's very tempting to let this demand guide training development and delivery, resulting in training that's littered with way too many training targets and ultimately doesn't work. Following this path most likely results in powerful outcomes like relieving administrative pressure or meeting some training quota. Remember, if it didn't result in some sort of valued outcome, people wouldn't do it! This leaves countless examples of workforce, college, and internet training modules where the desire to get everyone trained in a short period of time regardless of how is causing people to ignore the most important outcome. It is overshadowing learning.

Checking a Box versus Checking for Learning

Once you've weeded out the behaviors that either aren't really important enough for training or that are better suited for another type of antecedent, then it becomes a question of how much to train at once. A lecture or short presentation, followed by a quiz, will give you enough to claim that the training for the topic is complete. If this is the standard, it's relatively easy to cover a lot of training in a short amount of time—but there's a cost that will be obvious to you by this point. This doesn't mean that lectures and short presentations are bad (they aren't), or that quizzes don't have a purpose (they do). What is missing is acknowledgement of the learner. Science tells us that learning requires responding. The more opportunities to offer responses and get feedback on them, the greater the learning. So training systems that are quick but offer limited opportunities for the trainee to perform and get feedback (like that quiz you take at the end) will not produce learning. And if your training isn't producing learning, then the only thing it's really doing is checking a box for administrative purposes. Look at your primary outcome for training—it should have at least something to do with learning!

Organizing Training Content

How you organize your training content should be based on four variables, all of which can affect the efficacy of your training and the reach of your training's impact.

#1. Search for Criticality

The content driving your training endeavors can come from a number of places. Maybe you've been handed a list of new mandatory education targets, or perhaps the content is standardized based on common requirements of the teachers in your state. If there's flexibility, consider whether these training targets actually *need* to be trained. We know this might seem a little counterintuitive given that it's the job of a school leader to ensure skills are built where skill deficits exist. But how valuable is the particular skill to day-to-day work activities? If you don't weed out the elements that don't matter, it can be difficult for teachers to tell the difference between the critical parts of the training and the parts they should be passingly familiar with. This can be extremely frustrating and cause them to undervalue the entirety of the training.

If a particular target doesn't fit within your training priorities, don't worry; it doesn't mean it will be ignored. There are other ways to get the performance you're looking for. Prompts, like quick reference guides and job aids, are antecedents just like training is. Teachers have a lot of rules, names, procedures, acronyms, etc., that they supposedly need to know off the top of their heads. But do they? Which ones are used most frequently? Which ones are better suited for a quick reference guide? Some of these rules and procedures might change so frequently that you'll spend more time rebuilding and retraining than you did with your initial onboarding. A well-designed checklist or reference guide can help employees perform accurately without wasting resources on teaching the hundreds of acronyms they might face on the job.

In his book *The First 90 Days*, Michael Watkins emphasizes the importance of capitalizing on the initial three critical months of employment. The faster you get a new hire on the job, happy, and productive, the faster you, and the employee, will see their value. New teachers and staff can have a large impact during this critical time period, and your training systems have a lot to do with it.

You need to give your training a fighting chance to build the necessary skills for an individual to succeed and sustain those skills over time. If a skill isn't going to be used often, there's no reinforcement in the environment to keep this behavior strong in the person's repertoire. It will eventually fade away.

Differentiating critical areas from those that are good to know but not integral to performance is an important step in organizing your training content. For instance, you might wish to train employees on how your organization was formed, why it delivers the services that it does, and why things operate the way they do. But prioritizing things like *how* to deliver the service over things like *why* the service is delivered enables the employee to access more reinforcers and become more productive more quickly.

Your path to building good work habits starts by training the right behaviors and making the individual aware of the positive consequences associated with those behaviors. Many professions, including behavior analysis, will survey professionals in the field with the goal of producing essential training content. The results can lead to job analysis studies and other assessments geared toward finding critical areas that all practitioners in the field need to know. Prioritizing those critical behaviors in your training will save time and money and help maximize the value of your training.

#2. Break Down Complex Skills into Smaller Component Skills

Just as you can save a great deal of time and resources by training the *right* behaviors, you can also maximize the efficiency of your training by looking at the *order* in which you're covering these behaviors.

By first identifying your targeted outcomes, you've set yourself up to separate the critical behavior pinpoints (remember, behaviors that are specific and measurable) you'll need to train to hit those targets. General conversation about behavior often involves a focus on a descriptor or process like "building relationships," "getting students engaged," or "showing passion." These are larger composite skills that are made up of the individual components (behaviors) that you've targeted for development in your training. The process of breaking down a complex skill into the component skills targeted for training is called a *task analysis*. Car mechanics initially need to know the key parts of the car, the function of each applicable mechanism, the steps to fixing various potential issues, and so on in order to effectively complete their duties. Teachers need to know what type of responding they want from students (e.g., choral, individualized, written), how to prompt these opportunities using well-planned instructions and questions, and how to respond to the students with feedback and reinforcement as they're participating in order to effectively build student engagement. These behaviors are all critical to an end goal of learning a larger complex skill. Breaking down these skills will help refine your training and ensure that nothing is being missed.

The trainee's workday should be better after completing your training.

#3. Find Your Behavioral Cusps

The component skills identified through your task analysis will help direct your training efforts, building both the individual and the more complex composite skills. If we dig around in our science toolbox, there is another behavioral concept that helps select training targets. These targets take things a step further, opening doors to *new* behaviors and *new* opportunities. They're referred to as *behavioral cusps*.

In 2001, a pair of researchers from Western Michigan University published a model for selecting target behaviors based on the concept of behavioral cusps (Fuqua

& Bosch). The more criteria a behavior meets, the stronger it is as a training target, and the more you and the performer will experience a return on investment.

1. Does the skill you're training help the person access reinforcers and desired environments? We learn letters, numbers, words, and other reading components in order to engage in reading activities throughout our lives. Reading is an important behavioral cusp in that it helps us access other reinforcers that will in turn help build new behaviors. Reading means you can now access fun books and magazines, and eventually even that book on Deliberate Coaching that will help you in your new vice principal or instructional coaching job!
2. Does the skill help other people? Training proper communication strategies is an important behavioral cusp that has a significant impact on all parties. Teachers and coaches in education have a broad impact on those around them. A teacher learning how to properly communicate student concerns with parents can help the teacher get the type of parent support needed for the student to succeed while also helping the student and peers working with the student. The parent will see how communicating and adhering to teacher instructions helps the child and, in turn, can start seeing the value of working more with the teacher.
3. Does the skill benefit the organization or community? Of the many behaviors targeted during leadership training, the ability to provide precise, sincere, and consistent positive reinforcement is the most critical. Why? It's not only good for the leader providing the reinforcement (leading to improved relationships) and the direct reports receiving the reinforcement (who learn faster and develop improved self-esteem), but it adds positivity and growth to any system. The better the skill fits within the classroom, the more likely the skill is to have sustained value that transfers beyond the classroom doors.
4. Does the skill help generate other desired behaviors? Schools use code systems to publicly communicate various messages to staff. Knowing and reacting appropriately to these codes is an important behavioral cusp because it has a range of uses. It can help you avoid dangerous situations and protect students, it can tell you where to go and when you're needed, and it can show you what to avoid so as not to make things worse. Along with benefiting the staff and students, learning these codes can generate new behaviors (what to do when you hear the code), new opportunities for reinforcement (for following the code), and new situational rules (what happens in code-related situations).
5. Does the new skill replace an ineffective, inefficient, or otherwise inappropriate skill? If your training is to serve as a solution to a performance

problem, your behavioral cusp could be a new, more desired skill. Perhaps teachers are following the wrong procedure, cutting corners that result in costly or dangerous errors that negatively impact student achievement, or are using an outdated method that takes too much time and yields fewer results. Training new skills to replace these costly skills can add significant value.

Train people how to ask for a fish when hungry and they'll be able to ask for and maybe even receive a fish. Focus on a behavioral cusp and they'll know how to catch their own fish and perhaps feed other people if necessary.

"The difference between ordinary and extraordinary is practice."
—Vladimir Horowitz

#4. Focus on Fluency

So you've separated your need-to-know skills from your good-to-know skills and prioritized the order in which to train them. If they're critical, then you want expert-level responses that result from your training. You want them responding fluently (quickly and accurately).

Say you're a beginning guitar player learning a new song. You wish to wow your friends and family at the local holiday party by showing off your improved chops. You commit, get people excited to see what you've been learning, maybe even brag a bit because you've made some fast progress on learning your fingerings. As you start to practice, however, your nerves turn into intense fear as you realize that you don't yet have the tools to play a whole song, and your performance might be a colossal embarrassment. A song is a combination of a number of component skills like identifying different chord structures, forming chords on the fretboard, moving from one chord to another (quickly), strumming in rhythm, and doing it all so seamlessly that you can lead a group in an off-pitch rendition of "Jingle Bells" without skipping a beat. So you spend every waking hour deliberately practicing each component skill one by one, then in combination, until you can do it. You become accurate and you become fast—you become fluent enough to take your guitar and ugly Christmas sweater to the party with confidence.

One valuable lesson you might consider when developing training at your school is that if you teach component skills to fluency, more complex composite skills will occur more quickly and easily. If you can spell and sound out words fluently, you're more likely to pick up reading and writing. If you're fluent in the parts of a cell, you're more likely to excel when teaching students these parts and troubleshooting student barriers. As you design your training, the type of responses you'll require from your participants during training (e.g., fluency versus mastery) can dictate the success of your training.

Behavioral Skills Training

Fortunately, there is a simple yet well-researched process for developing skills that incorporates many of these strategies. This process is called behavioral skills training (BST). In short, it employs instruction, modeling, rehearsal, and feedback as a system for developing a variety of performance skills. Reid and Parsons (2006) suggest the following steps:

1. Specify skills to be taught (declarative knowledge)
2. Provide training participants with a written summary of skills specified (declarative knowledge)
3. Verbally describe the skills with a rationale (the why!) for targeting the skills for training (declarative knowledge)
4. Physically demonstrate the skills for the participants (declarative knowledge)
5. Observe the participants as they practice the targeted skills (procedural knowledge)
6. Provide corrective or supportive feedback to the participants based on their demonstration of the skills (procedural knowledge)
7. Continue steps 4, 5, and 6 until the participants can perform the targeted skills correctly (procedural knowledge)

At this point you might be thinking, "How the heck can we give a training where participants get to practice *and* receive a steady stream of feedback?" This is a good thought. Classroom models of training are great for accommodating a large group of people but are often poor at providing them opportunities for adequate practice and feedback. The solution: peer feedback.

As you know, skills are a chain of behaviors that lead to a desired outcome. This chain can be broken down into a set of smaller written steps or components as we outlined in the task analysis and is exemplified by Reid and Parsons's seven steps for developing skills. Once these steps are listed, they can be used by participants to guide and provide feedback to one another as a cooperative learning strategy.

Let's unpack this a bit further to demonstrate task analysis as an extremely valuable tool. In fact, this tool might be considered a behavioral cusp for both teachers and coaches as it can be used to achieve meaningful outcomes under a variety of conditions. Imagine a trainer was teaching participants to use *behavior-specific praise* to improve academic achievement. For example, "Johnny, you got the math problem right because you remembered to carry over the one. Nice job!" Or perhaps the focus was on improving behavior, "Johnny, thanks for raising your hand and waiting to be called on before speaking." Behavior-specific praise is a skill that can be broken down into a series of components and steps. Once these are broken down into steps, they can be written on a sheet of paper as a checklist and used by participants to score one another regarding their declarative knowledge (i.e., can they state the steps) and their procedural knowledge (i.e., can they perform the steps) during practices.

There are many cooperative learning strategies for increasing feedback and engaging learners during instructor-led training models. Kagan (2009) lists a variety of these strategies that can be employed with both students and educators. Here is how the process of a task analysis might look using what Kagan calls the Inside-Outside Circle:

Performance Feedback Task Activity: Describing Key Elements of the Skill	
Description: Teachers rotate in concentric circles to face new partners for sharing, quizzing, or problem solving. Teachers use the Describing Skill performance task sheet to interview each other in the Inside-Outside Circle.	
Setup: Presenter provides the definitions, role plays, and allows the teachers to score the presenter using the performance feedback sheet under the P that is highlighted in yellow.	
Step 1	Participants are asked to stand up with their Describing Skill sheet and form pairs. One teacher from each pair moves to form one large circle facing outward. The remaining teachers find and face their partners (class now stands in two concentric circles).
Step 2	Teacher exchanges their Describing Skill sheet with their partner, then asks their partner to describe the skills without looking at the sheet. Participants score each other and return their Describing Skill sheets to each other.
Step 3	Trainer directs inside-circle participants to rotate clockwise to a new partner. Trainer may call rotation numbers (e.g., "Rotate three ahead").
Step 4	Presenter asks participants to find another partner and repeat until the Describing Skill sheet is completed and participants have reached established performance goals.

Figure 7.1.

This process provides a safe way for participants to practice and receive precise feedback through a task analyzed checklist. It can include a question about the why, as illustrated in the Describing Behavior-Specific Praise table. While this example only lists six intervals beyond the initial P (presenter) column, the number can be increased based on the complexity of the task to allow for more repetitions and feedback. The goal might be for the participant to accurately describe the steps three times in a row before moving on to the next step of actually performing the skill.

P		1	2	3	4	5	6	Describing Behavior-Specific Praise
	Y							Teacher should make positive comment about specific behavior immediately following the behavior.
	N							
	Y							Teacher should align the behavior with progress toward a goal.
	N							
	Y							Teacher should appear sincere (smile!).
	N							
	Y							Effectively used when teachers are trying to increase or strengthen a desired behavior.
	N							

Figure 7.2.

Once the teacher can describe the skill accurately, they should be provided the opportunity to practice it using the same process. The Performance Feedback Task Activity table shows what that process might look like. Remember, the previous Describing Behavior-Specific Praise activity requires the performer to *describe* the skills, whereas the process that follows it requires the performer to actually demonstrate the skill while the peer checks off which components were implemented correctly, and which were implemented incorrectly. By engaging peers in the process of measurement and feedback, performance across the entire group is accelerated.

Performance Feedback Task Activity—Describing Key Elements of the Skill	
Description: Teachers rotate in concentric circles to face new partners for sharing, quizzing, or problem solving. Teachers use the Performing Skill performance task sheet to score and provide feedback to each other in the Inside-Outside Circle.	
Setup: Presenter provides the definitions, role plays, and allows the participants to score the presenter using the performance feedback sheet under the P that is highlighted in yellow.	
Step 1	Participants are asked to stand up with their Performing Skill sheet and form pairs. One teacher from each pair moves to form one large circle facing outward. The remaining teachers find and face their partners (class now stands in two concentric circles).
Step 2	Teacher exchanges their Performing Skill sheet with their partner, and the trainer provides the participants with a scenario highlighting a student behaving in a way that a teacher would like to see repeated.
Step 3	The participant asks their partner to demonstrate the skills based on the scenario provided, and without looking at the sheet. Participants score each other, then return their Performing Skill sheets to each other. Trainer directs inside-circle participants to rotate clockwise to a new partner. Trainer may call rotation numbers (e.g., "Rotate three ahead").
Step 4	Presenter asks participants to find another partner and repeat until the Performing Skill sheet is completed based on an established goal (e.g., performing each step correctly three times in a row).

Figure 7.3.

And here is an example of the corresponding performance checklist. Except this checklist is intended to measure performance or application of procedural knowledge as opposed to describing the skill or declarative knowledge.

P		1	2	3	4	5	6	Performing Behavior-Specific Praise
	Y							Teacher made positive comment about specific behavior immediately following the behavior.
	N							
	Y							Teacher aligned the behavior with progress toward a goal.
	N							
	Y							Teacher smiled.
	N							
	Y							Teacher explained it should be used when attempting to increase or strengthen a desired behavior.
	N							

Figure 7.4.

In another example, the trainer teaches participants how to use an attention signal. Here is what that task-analyzed performance sheet might look like.

P		1	2	3	4	5	6	Attention Signal
	Y							Teacher used an auditory prompt (e.g., "Your attention please").
	N							
	Y							Teacher used a visual prompt (e.g., hand raised).
	N							
	Y							Teacher waited for student(s) to stop, look, and listen before providing direction.
	N							
	Y							Teacher explained the attention signal should be used to gain student attention prior to providing a new directive to the class.
	N							

Figure 7.5.

Practice and feedback is where the rubber meets the road in training when the ultimate goal is to develop skills. We're probably starting to sound like a broken record here, but that's okay. Without practice and feedback, training is a waste of precious time and money. Using behavioral skills training and engaging participants in performance-based peer feedback as illustrated in the previous example is a powerful approach to ensuring that participants actually walk away with the ability to apply skills within the school.

Conditional Knowledge

In business, good executive coaches understand that talent development involves a process of instructing, modeling, and observing paired with constant feedback to shape the skill. This is the development of the declarative and procedural knowledge discussed in chapter 2. These coaches also understand that transferring skills learned in practice to actual performance in the organization is critical to success. Some leaders who make amazing speeches and drop inspirational quotes at the annual staff meeting will regularly demonstrate critical errors in leadership that impact their bottom line—they talk the talk but fail to walk the walk.

Sometimes poor performance can be linked to failure of skills to generalize from one environment to another, as conditional knowledge wasn't nurtured during the talent-development process. People know the why and the how, but they don't behave the right way at the right time.

Conditional knowledge is developed experientially; it allows the performer to understand the when while strengthening the why and how in the context of the work environment. It connects the skills and knowledge learned through deliberate practice and allows the learner to apply this knowledge within various aspects of the job. In teaching or school leadership, conditional knowledge allows the educators to follow school improvement plans as they apply the right technique at the right time. From a behaviorist point of view, this knowledge can be represented across multiple people and tasks through a series of "if-thens." You remember, those "metacontingencies" discussed in chapter 1: "If this happens, then I will do that."

For example, in various businesses, good talent developers often use performance-based scenarios or *simulations* to allow their employees the opportunity to safely apply learned skills under conditions that closely mimic the actual work environment. Under these conditions, performance can be assessed and shaped by the trainers as they engage in actual work activities during role plays. Simulations offer a powerful strategy for increasing the likelihood that performers will be effective on the job.

Business mogul Richard Branson was quoted as saying, "Clients do not come first. Employees come first. If you take care of your employees, they will take care of the clients." If districts and schools wish to help leaders and educators reach their greatest potential, teacher preparation and training programs must focus more on helping them perform to their potential by providing effective talent development that requires rehearsal under "fight like" conditions. Training is absolutely critical for equipping educators with the skills they need to be successful. But talent development doesn't end in the training sessions. An effective approach must help the educator to transfer the skills they learn into the actual school—a Deliberate Coaching process.

Use It Wisely

Training, in all its forms and functions, is first and foremost an antecedent. It is used to set people up to succeed, providing each trainee a repertoire critical to their job function. It can both *motivate* learners and *guide* learners. Reflect back on the concept of using training to address performance problems. If there is a true need for training, then you should be able to link the training to something meaningful to the individual or school, something that makes it worthwhile and fixes the problem. If learning is fun, interesting, and presented in a way that demonstrates value, then the trainee will want to learn. This is a critical feature of any skill-building system, be it training, coaching, or some related initiative. It builds exemplars with strong productive work habits and helps create an organizational culture of success. You want people seeking out your training because they've found it adds value and fixes something they see as broken.

With typical training, the burden of learning is unjustly placed on the individual learner. They should participate in training, regardless of why it's being administered, because it's their job and that's what they're paid for. But while job requirements will get them in the door, the training is doomed to fail if that's the only reason they think they're participating in training. If motivation during training is low, then you shouldn't expect the motivation to *use* whatever was trained to be much higher.

If you want teachers to apply your training properly, then you need to show objective impact, particularly impact during those times it's being used in the way that you want it to be used. What does the teacher need to succeed in a positive and efficient way? And how will the training help the teacher to do this? Maybe a teacher has struggled to manage some disruptive students, which impacts the progress of those students and others in the classroom. If you can link the training you're providing with the progress the teacher is making in this area, then you're showing measurable impact—you're showing value. Without measurable impact after training, the training will appear to be useless, and if training isn't the solution (that is, if the individual can already demonstrate everything being trained), then the training may very well *be* useless. Why do it if the training adds nothing of note to the individual or the classroom? The burden of learning is on the trainer, those building the training, and those making decisions about how to use the training. Those are the individuals responsible for motivation, and motivation is what drives learning and subsequent performance.

School training systems should be given a chance to add value to the teachers and staff participating in them. If not, the training days at your school, and those working hard to build and deliver those trainings, risk losing value. Here are a few things to consider when looking to maximize the impact of training services on performance problems.

#1. Rule Out Environmental Barriers

As part of a 2005 study on performance assessment, store managers at a chain of sandwich shops stated that one of their top priorities was to get their staff to offer promotional stamps when a customer purchased a sandwich (Rodriguez et al., 2005). This was important to the stores as it helped drive future business, but the staff was struggling. A key discovery made during the study: the machine that dispensed the promotional stamps was broken.

When you look at the many organizational assessments researched and utilized over the years, one recommendation remains clear: don't be quick to assume it's the performer's fault. Malfunctioning equipment, vague or nonexistent policies and procedures, and other systems barriers can impact performance as much or more than a lack of knowledge and a lack of consequences. If the teacher knows how to run a program, but there are no materials for that program in the classroom, no amount of training will fix this problem. Rule this out first.

#2. Find the True Cause of the Performance Problem

You've ruled out that there are no environmental or process barriers hindering performance, so now what? Now we get back to our ABCs. When deciding whether training is the answer to a performance problem, see if the individual can demonstrate the task and demonstrate it at a high level. If so, it's not a knowledge or skills issue. Since the fundamental purpose of training is to address knowledge and skill deficits, spending time on training in this case would produce little to no benefit. You'd be better off looking to use other antecedents, such as reminders or checklists, and providing effective and consistent feedback. If the individual cannot demonstrate the skill, then your training can be used as a reactive solution, specifically targeting the missing skill set.

#3. Identify Your Proactive-Training Needs

When used as a proactive skill builder as opposed to a reactive one, training systems target a seemingly blank canvas. Again, based on either assessment or assumption, training provides knowledge and skills that individuals either don't have in their repertoire or don't have at the target level. The goal here is to help people understand what the leaders and training instructor deem integral to success given a new role or new change initiative. This might be directed toward using a new process or piece of equipment, getting new hires up to speed on critical procedures, seeing that key individuals know how to fix an impending problem, or another area of skill-building priority. The purpose behind proactive training is to provide a repertoire that they don't already possess. The key for trainers is to properly identify that repertoire and relay the value of this skill set during the training.

One Last Point on Trial and Error

As you look around your school and your life outside of work, you'll find there is no shortage of opportunities to use training to address performance deficits. Assessing the cause of the performance problem can save you a lot of time, money, and frustration. However, you might still be on the fence about the problem of relying too much on trial and error in your selection of performance solutions. Yes, moving toward a strategic use of training and other solutions means moving away from a proven and familiar methodology. Yes, it takes time to accommodate the trials, and there is a cost to the errors. Nonetheless, the solution might still appear at the end of this path. So what's the harm in guessing?

Three outcomes can result from discarding your scientific know-how, none of which provide optimal long-term solutions from a leadership perspective.

- *Outcome #1—you guess right.* This is your best-case scenario. You find that training happened to work and do the same thing the next time, hoping that you guess right again. But if your guess is wrong the second time and it's not a knowledge or skill issue, you'll be back to square one. Good leaders know why their leadership initiatives worked and can replicate results.
- *Outcome #2—you make it worse.* Suppose you have a select group of highly skilled, well-trained teachers who are working hard to hit their student-progress measures despite faulty equipment, missing materials, absent teacher assistants, and other issues out of their control. Individually, they're going above and beyond. However, lower performers are bringing down the success of the school as a whole, and as a result you force the entire group to get retrained on the basics of teaching standards and classroom goals. By assuming a knowledge or skill deficit of the entire group, you've punished the high performance of your exemplars. The end result is a group of low-performing teachers, still performing below standard after the needless retraining, as well as exemplars who feel ignored and disrespected, leading to declining performance across the board.
- *Outcome #3—nothing happens.* You might not have fixed the problem, but you also didn't make it worse. You lost some time and money, and your teachers and staff returned from training to the same situation they were in before.

A Framework for Performance Improvement

The science of behavior offers a level of precision that seeks out the causes of behavior in order to maximize the effective leadership tools you have in your repertoire, including the proper use of valuable training and professional or talent development systems. These are evidence-based tools to help you assess, manage, and sustain any issues related to learning and performance. A key discovery in this science is that behavior occurs or doesn't occur for a reason. This reason, whatever it is, should guide performance-improvement initiatives like training. Without a reliable understanding of *why* a particular performance problem has occurred, you are lacking the most critical piece of information—information that should be guiding not just your training but all your leadership efforts. Without knowing the cause of the performance problem, you're losing many of the advantages of a scientific analysis of learning and performance. By skipping the sound practice that has been proven to produce faster and longer-lasting performance improvements for your school personnel, you're not allowing yourself to truly maximize training and other leadership solutions.

We're offering a consistent and replicable framework. New behaviors are trained by presenting the right instructions, training materials, and other antecedents to get these skills going and using positive reinforcement to accelerate the learning, effectively building these skills into a person's repertoire. Select these training targets carefully. If you do this, you can maximize the time spent training and provide real value to the learner. The trainee's workday should be better after completing your training. Can they now do a job they couldn't do before? Can they do it more productively? Is their job easier? Can they and others see the value in these newly trained skills? You can find great value in your training via a quick examination of how you're prioritizing critical training content.

So how should you use the training systems you and your team have worked so hard to build? Give learners the tools they need to be successful. Take into account that the ABCs of our science requires antecedents, and as trainers we're responsible for one of the most important of those. And, perhaps most importantly, make sure the problem justifies the use of training.

Training is a valuable necessity in every person's life. We just need to capture and maximize that value by appreciating how and when training is used. If a coach uses tools like training and coaching properly and people see the value of the coaching, then more people will want the coach around and benefit from what the coach has to offer.

CHAPTER 8

TRAINING VERSUS COACHING

If you don't have clarity of ideas, you're just communicating sheer sound.

—Yo-Yo Ma

There's a wide array of literature on coaching, ranging from evidence-based journals and books by well-known authors to internet articles and posts by experts in the field. If you take a step back and look at the way we're talking about these topics, you'll quickly discover that the discipline of coaching is still developing and lacks a well-grounded definition.

Despite the contradictions, we found that many definitions of coaching overlap. Words like *supporting*, *training*, *partnering*, *helping*, *modeling*, *feedback*, and *goal setting* are commonly used to describe coaching behaviors. And descriptions like *unlocking potential*, *skill development*, *goal achievement*, and *performance improvement* are often used to illustrate outcomes associated with coaching.

Many of these same descriptions sometimes overlap with definitions associated with mentoring and training. In fact, it's not uncommon for coaches to be referred to as trainers or mentors and vice versa. But we're not concerned with titles so much as the impact of the strategies and when they're most valuable. If you apply coaching or mentoring as an intervention when training is needed, the results will fall far short of the desired outcome. As such, we think it's important to delineate these concepts so it's clear when coaching is appropriate and when it's not.

Mentoring, Training, and Coaching

Mentor, *trainer*, and *coach* are roles somebody fulfills, whereas *training*, *mentoring*, and *coaching* are the approaches or tools used by trainers, mentors, and coaches. Each of these approaches is aimed at helping people improve, each borrows from the same skill sets, and each can be used by somebody regardless of their title. And, *topographically*, each of these approaches looks similar as it is applied in the moment. For example, each uses feedback as a tool for improvement.

We propose that the difference between mentoring, training, and coaching lies in different variables such as timescale and context; however, the most important factor that discriminates these approaches can be found in the purpose or *functionality* of each. This is an important distinction because *topography* and *function* are very different things. Where topography tells us what a behavior looks like, function tells us why it occurs (Cooper, Heron, & Heward, 2007).

Say somebody turns the light switch on a lamp. If the person is turning the light on, their behavior *functions* to increase the amount of light in the room. If they are turning it off, then their behavior *functions* to decrease the amount of light in the room. In both cases their topography or form looks exactly the same: turning the light switch. But each behavior serves a vastly different purpose, or function.

Another behavior with different potential purposes is waving. If somebody sees a friend, they might wave to say hello. If they're at a restaurant and would like to request a refill of water, they might wave as a signal for the waiter to come to the table. In both cases, waving (the topography) looks exactly the same, but they each function for different reasons.

The overlapping descriptions associated with mentoring, training, and coaching are similar. Many of the behaviors connected with these approaches, like feedback and modeling, *look* the same. The differences in *function*, paired with timescales and contexts, are what separate them.

Mentoring

There are many definitions of mentoring, typically reflective of a personal, long-term relationship that deepens over time and has a ripple effect toward personal and career goals. From an academic organizational perspective (Erdem & Aytemur, 2008):

> Mentoring can be described as the provision of guidance, knowledge, opportunities and support by a senior experienced member of an organization (the mentor) for a younger, inexperienced member (the protégé) for as long as required to help the advancement of a protégé.

Where training is often a formal time-based and skill-oriented process that functions to develop specific skill sets, mentoring is relationship-oriented, typically *functioning* to accomplish general long-term goals related to personal or professional success (Erdem, & Aytemur, 2008; Megginson & Clutterbuck, 2005).

Mentoring can be both formal and informal. In either case, it often involves establishing long-term goals, determining actions, reviewing progress, and making adjustments. For example, in education, a seasoned principal might use mentoring to help a teacher who has the goal of becoming an assistant principal improve her leadership skills.

Good mentors employ a variety of strategies for helping their mentees, including training if they see the need and possess the prerequisite knowledge and skills. Similarly, good mentors might serve as coaches and use "coaching" to help their mentees accomplish goals. We'll talk more about coaching shortly. But first, let's take a functional look at training so it can be differentiated from mentoring and coaching.

Training

Training is commonly understood as a process intended to develop competency of a defined population for a specific purpose. BusinessDictionary.com defines it as "Organized activity aimed at imparting information and/or instructions to improve the recipient's performance or to help him or her attain a required level of knowledge or skill."

In general, training is an approach that occurs over an allotted time period, in a designated area or areas. It focuses on what needs to be done and why it needs to be done, and it involves strategies like instruction, modeling, and rehearsal to meet a standard of proficiency. From a functional perspective, training is skill-oriented and *functions* as a means of helping a performer develop a skill until it can be demonstrated proficiently and independently.

For example, if a teacher is learning the theory and techniques for asking rigorous questions, she might receive training during a professional-development day in their school's designated training area. The teacher's goal is to acquire the knowledge and skills to correctly ask rigorous questions within the classroom. Under these conditions the trainer might explain the theory behind rigorous questions and academic achievement, model how to ask questions, and require participants to practice by asking questions with a partner as they are provided feedback. Ideally, this occurs until the teacher is able to perform the task independently.

Once this happens, the teacher is ready to be coached. But what is coaching from a functional perspective, and when is it appropriate?

Coaching

According to the *Oxford Advanced Learner's Dictionary* (2011), the term "coaching" refers to "the process of training somebody to play a sport, to do a job better or to improve a skill." In the business world, it's been described as "a training method in which a more experienced or skilled individual provides an employee with advice and guidance intended to help develop the individual's skills, performance, and career" (Society for Human Resource Management, 2017).

If these definitions sound similar to those we shared regarding mentoring and training, it's because they are. This is part of the problem. As you can see, coaching is often conflated with concepts associated with training (e.g., skill acquisition) and mentoring (e.g., career development). While these definitions and descriptions aren't bad, they muddy the water.

While training helps *develop* skills, coaching as we define it involves time-based, task-oriented behaviors which *function to transfer a performer's previously acquired skills into the natural environment.* In other words, coaching picks up where training leaves off. When successful, it results in sustainable performance and achievement of targeted outcomes. As such, its timescale can be far shorter than that of mentoring.

Coaching can come in different packages depending on the conditions and the needs of the performer. For example, it might include immediate feedback, video feedback, written feedback, modeling, measurement, and so on.

Where training and mentoring tend to occur in sterile environments outside the natural setting, coaching can occur under both simulated (outside the natural setting) or in-vivo (live) conditions as part of the transference process. From a behavioral perspective, coaching should focus primarily on successfully applying skills within the work environment and helping performers get in contact with naturally occurring positive reinforcement through feedback and measurement. For example, it might help a teacher to see that students are learning more, students are misbehaving less, or the job has become easier. This will increase the likelihood the teacher will use this skill in the future. However, if a performer does not yet possess the prerequisite skills required to complete the task that would get them in touch with naturally occurring positive reinforcement, then coaching isn't the appropriate intervention—training is.

Training and Coaching in Action

Let's return to the example of fighting from our discussion on behavioral skills training. When developing fighters, good coaches have two primary repertoires: training and coaching. To clearly illustrate the difference, let's explore how good combat sports coaches develop skills through training and help the fighter transfer these skills into the fight through coaching (Gavoni & Edmonds, 2014).

1. *New skill sets.* Under conditions where fighters are learning a new skill set, coaches should create routines that allow for safe, deliberate practice. Throwing a fighter into the ring and expecting them to fight successfully is counterproductive. As a student in elementary school, you wouldn't go straight from learning where Portugal is to having a geography test on all of Europe, right?

   Fighting routines include drills like bag work, mitts, shadowboxing, or any noncontact drill that allows for deliberate, high-repetition practice. During these training sessions, coaches should strive to provide frequent feedback directly related to the specific skills. When developing new skill sets, it's important that the fighter use repetition to build fluency. Similarly, it's important for educators to have the opportunity to build fluency in skills through safe practice.
2. *Emerging skill sets.* Under conditions where fighters are demonstrating emerging skills related to a targeted skill set, coaches should create routines that involve low-impact, controlled sparring drills to allow for deliberate practice. For example, if a coach has been teaching a defensive skill that the fighter can perform without prompting, the coach might have two fighters spar lightly (i.e., controlled fighting). Under these conditions, the coach would allow one fighter to lead with offense and the other to respond with the targeted defensive skill. This allows the fighter to experience high repetitions of the targeted defense while allowing the coach to refine skills through observation and feedback under conditions that are closer to actual fighting. It will also allow the fighter to experience success. As the fighter who's learning the combo moves closer to proficiency, the coach can allow both fighters to increase the intensity during controlled sparring.

   This illustration would be akin to the use of simulations whereby educators were focused on performing a targeted skill under "classroom-like" conditions that included the use of role play.
3. *Proficiency with skill sets.* The ultimate goal of a boxing coach is to equip fighters with a skill set that they can perform effectively during sparring, and eventually in a fight. When a fighter becomes proficient during controlled sparring drills, coaches should systematically begin permitting the fighter to add additional punches to the combo. During this phase, coaches should continue to observe and provide feedback, with the

> objective of fading their direct coaching of this skill until the fighter can implement the skill independently and fluently.
>
> Similarly, educators who initially were focused on performing just one targeted skill during a simulation now might be directed to add in more skills as they begin to independently perform to targeted standards.

This three-step process illustrates how a coach can use training behaviors to develop new skill sets (e.g., drills), and then employ coaching behavior (e.g., providing feedback during sparring or simulated conditions) to allow for transference into the natural setting. In addition to developing the skills and performance of a fighter, coaches in boxing typically serve as mentors, as they often leverage their relationship to support fighters both personally and professionally.

To recap: The process of developing performance of a teacher or any educator follows a very similar path. A teacher might first learn new skill sets through the training on things like classroom management and curriculum design. Once they're proficient, they should receive coaching to refine and effectively apply those skills during simulations and eventually in the classroom. While this happens on a relatively short timescale, a new teacher often welcomes regular mentoring to aid with the attainment of long-term goals.

Hopefully we've been able to clear up some of the confusion associated with these concepts, particularly in relation to coaching. We will continue to talk about effective training methods in later chapters, as it should be clear by now that good coaching can't occur without good training.

Simulations to Foster Coaching Interactions

Let's pretend you have the ability to take a fictional trip back in time, to a fictional sporting event. As a huge basketball fan (bear with us here), you decide to travel to 1891 to witness the first basketball game as well as the preparation for it. So you put in the appropriate date and coordinates, then find yourself transported to Springfield College, the birthplace of basketball (Naismith, 1941). After doing a little inquiry, you discover that two teams will be playing, so you make arrangements to observe them as they prepare.

The first team, the Memorizers, is busy completing multiple drills to perfect shooting and drilling ability. You watch as a group of young men line-up to take shot after shot from a designated spot and are impressed by how often the ball goes into the basket (literally a peach basket). In another group, young men are taking turns running up and down the court and dribbling a large round ball. Their movement is primitive compared to the NBA players of today, but you appreciate their dedication to developing their skills, as you believe practice makes perfect, and you marvel at the high rate of shots the players are making.

After two hours of watching nonstop training on various skills, you venture out in search of the opposing team, the Simulators. As you find a spot to observe off to the side, you're struck by a stark difference. While one group of players is deliberately practicing skills as the Memorizers did, the other group is playing what looks like a practice game on the other end of the court as a coach circles like a shark and gives various players feedback.

You watch them run around awkwardly (by today's standards), missing far more shots than the groups you've witnessed standing at the line making practice shots, but still making a fair amount. As you think about it, you're surprised you didn't observe this method while watching the other team. After all, scrimmaging is a staple of modern-day sports.

The night of the game arrives, and you find yourself a spot on the wooden bleachers. As the teams come out, you wonder who will win the game. While the Simulators were able to scrimmage, the Memorizers engaged in far more repetition and appeared to have greater expertise, as their dribbling and shooting were more precise. This should be interesting.

The whistle blows, and the teams begin making their mark in history. The Memorizers are able to secure the ball first. The player dribbles down the court using the clean and precise technique all of the players displayed during their practice. The Memorizers fans scream in anticipation as he makes his way past half court. And then, suddenly, the Memorizers fans are silenced as the Simulators player steals the ball and passes it to his teammate, who then dribbles it down the court and scores the first point ever. Despite a steady stream of directives from their coaches, the Memorizers are never able to get into the game. Fast-forward to the end and the analog scoreboard reads 112–4.

So what happened? Well, since you've been reading this book up until this point, we think you've guessed it. While the Memorizers were able to acquire necessary skills, the skills were never properly transferred to actual play. While they effectively developed procedural knowledge (doing the right thing) through lots of repetition, they were never provided the opportunity to develop their conditional knowledge (doing the right thing *at the right time*).

We've been pretty clear about this. Coaching is about getting skills to transfer to the natural environment. Before one can be concerned with transfer, these skills must first be developed, and the Memorizers put a lot of effort into skill development through practice. However, the coaching they received during the game proved fruitless as they'd never engaged in the game-like practice employed by the Simulators. Though well intended, the Memorizers' coaches never provided them with the opportunity to rehearse their skills under "simulated" conditions that mirrored actual play.

As we've noted, there has been a call to action by many professionals who say we need to develop educators. In our eyes, one of the most effective ways to do this would be housing teacher-preparation programs in actual schools, allowing would-be teachers to practice critical instructional behaviors extensively, and then pairing them with master teachers who are trained in coaching and can help them transfer their skills into the classroom. Since this isn't likely to happen in the near future, the next best thing might be to create school- and classroom-like scenarios that allow educators to gain repetition in problem solving, decision-making, and application of these skills during *simulations*.

A simulation, or the imitation of the operation of a real-world process or system (Banks, Carson, Nelson, & Nicol, 2010), has been used across industries for years to develop effective performance in the workplace. Professionals in economics, medicine, flight, military, sports, and even weather employ both analog and computerized simulations to create conditions that allow for essential practice in a wide range of problem-solving and decision-making processes that they'll face in their respective fields.

Researchers have found that well-designed simulations improve decision-making and critical-thinking skills as well as teaching discipline-related concepts (Thompson & Dass, 2000). Moreover, participants in simulations frequently report high levels of engagement when simulations employ cooperative learning strategies (Johnson & Johnson, 1994).

Thankfully, simulations are increasingly being used in education, providing the opportunity for teachers and leaders to fill relevant experiential gaps by putting them in virtual school or classroom situations (Baidee & Kaufman, 2014; Cruickshank, 1988). You can simulate things like how to respond to student questions, how to break down a lesson, or how to identify the cause for low student achievement. Like scrimmaging in sports, good simulations allow educators to practice while experiencing the consequences of a wide range of decisions. Moreover, they provide the opportunity for coaching to occur as participants can apply skills they've learned and receive feedback aimed at improving their application in the school.

How do you create a good simulation? It's actually not that difficult. While developing simulations is beyond the scope of this book, it starts by putting together a scenario. Here are a few more tips to get you started:

1. Use varied settings
2. Choose meaningful characters and determine role expectations
3. Determine the goals (i.e., what skills you want participants to use)
4. Determine how to deliver feedback
5. Establish measurable criteria for success

6. Create branching scenarios to illustrate consequences of decision-making
7. Determine how to debrief

We hope that we've piqued your interest in simulations. If you wish to explore the topic further, accelerating the transference of skills by fostering safe Deliberate Coaching opportunities, a quick internet search will yield lots of literature.

SECTION 3

THE DELIBERATE COACHING MODEL

CHAPTER 9

DELIBERATE COACHING

I don't look to jump over seven-foot bars. I look around for one-foot bars that I can step over.

—Warren Buffett

Welcome to section 3. We know we've thrown a lot at you. We also understand that change takes time, and we appreciate the need to start small. Find what will work for you to kick things off, knowing that you will most likely need to demonstrate the impact of this approach on teacher and coach performance to get large-scale buy-in. And that's fine, because this system is based on proven principles that have improved performance at schools, businesses, and countless other places for years. While you shouldn't expect yourself to remember everything you've read, we believe the stage for the Deliberate Coaching approach has been set. In this section we'll introduce you to a systematic approach and an arrangement of tools rooted in the behavior science that you learned about in section 2. These tools will provide you with a clear path to accelerating teacher performance.

Before we dive into the tools, let's take a look at a brief story to review some key concepts. As you read the story, put your behavioral detective hat on. See if you can find critical elements along the way that lead to the success of one group over the others. Moreover, reflect back on what you've learned in section 2 and try to figure out exactly why these elements help the group be successful. At the end of the story, we'll highlight these elements and give you a brief explanation that should serve to prime you for the rest of the book.

Climbing Mount Achievement

It's the end of June in North Carolina, and the sun slowly begins its ascent on the horizon. A small mountain sits prominently in the background as participants of Camp Achievement huddle around the base, chatting about various topics. The campers are marveling at what they've done so far, happy to have been chosen by their company to participate in this trip as a reward to their top salespeople. They feel fortunate that they were able to bring their family to the all-inclusive resort. Many are reflecting on their experiences in a four-week training course on hiking and mountain climbing. Most appear a bit anxious as they check their equipment, some seem to project confidence, and one group almost looks indifferent.

Today will mark the culmination of their hard work: reaching the peak of Mount Achievement, a task that is completed by two-thirds of the previous groups who have attempted the trek in the past. Their instructors have done a fine job training them. Through regular instruction, modeling, and rehearsal with feedback, the group as a whole has expressed confidence that they will reach the top easily. The trek should take approximately twenty hours with travel and rest if the group decides to follow the most frequently used path, though the instructors note that one group a couple of years ago made it to the top and bottom inside of fifteen hours.

The instructors have divided the group into three teams: Team Chill, Team Quick, and Team Deliberate. Each team has been provided all the necessary maps, equipment, and supplies. Based on the observations of the instructors, one member from each team has been appointed as the team leader. The team leader's main job up to now has been to facilitate planning meetings in preparation for the trek as well as act as a guide to ensure a safe journey up the mountain.

During these planning meetings, there were some stark differences between the teams. While the instructors had allotted four hours each week to plan, both Team Quick and Team Chill used very little of their planning time. In contrast, Team Deliberate could be seen reviewing maps, calculating times and distances, and even placing pins on the map that indicated landmarks. Based on the twenty-hour average, they knew precisely how long it should take to reach each one.

It's 7:00 a.m. The head instructor blows the horn to signal the start of their journey and tells everyone he'll see them in the main house to celebrate in three days. He also reminds them that if they have any trouble, they shouldn't hesitate to use the fully charged radios each of them has been provided.

It's apparent that each team has planned a different path up the side of the mountain as they all head in different directions. Team Chill's members, looking like seasoned hikers with their backpacks high on their shoulders, set off on a path leading to the right. They look back, give a final wave, and disappear from the view of the instructors. Out of view, the team leader quickly gathers his team around and says, "Okay, who's ready for a beer?" Everybody laughs, and they set off in the opposite direction of Mount Achievement. You see, Team Chill decided long ago that climbing Mount Achievement is of little value. They'd rather be back at the resort with their families enjoying food and drink. Nobody will know, so no harm done. They head off to return to their loved ones.

Team Quick has a different agenda. This team is highly competitive. Not only do they want to climb the mountain, but they want to break the record. As a team, they're determined to return inside of fourteen hours, an hour under the record. According to the maps, the most traveled path isn't a direct line to the top. So why take it? They've decided to take a less traveled path used by more experienced climbers. This path, they've projected, will shave off enough time to break the record.

Just two hours into the journey, some members begin to debate their direction as other paths become available. The team decides to split up into three smaller groups to travel down some of the paths. Since they have radios, they'll be able to radio one another and reunite the team once one of the groups has some indication that they're on the right path. One member, however, becomes so frustrated with the delay caused by the division and lack of direction that he leaves the group to return to the safety of the camp.

After another hour, they are discouraged. Though the path up the mountain seemed very clear on the maps and from the base, actually being on the mountain provides a whole new perspective. Unfortunately, Team Quick thought seeing the peak of the mountain through the trees was a good indicator that they were going in the right direction; however, after reaching dead ends on their paths, they are confronted with the error of their ways. Determined to reach it, the team decides their best and safest option is to return to the base of the mountain and follow the original path recommended by the instructors. They return, inform the instructors of their delay, and set off again. Team Quick reaches the mountaintop and returns in just over twenty-five hours.

Team Deliberate is taking a different approach, as they've spent a lot of time purposefully planning based on the information provided by the instructors. They've determined what path they'll take, why they'll take this path, who will carry what gear, when they'll stop for snacks, and when they'll camp for the night. Team Deliberate has even determined precisely what indicators will let them know they're moving in the right direction, as they've found landmarks in the maps and literature that will inform them of their progress up the mountain.

So they set off in good spirits at a measured pace. Not more than two hours into the journey, some members debate their direction as other paths become available. The team members, once very confident, are beginning to doubt themselves. After all, this is their first journey. The team leader, noticing that the pace has slowed and many members look discouraged, reviews his map and urges them to continue along the same route. "The big boulder should be just up ahead," he encourages them. "Once we come across it, we can be sure we're on the right path and approximately a tenth of the way up the mountain."

Soon enough, the team comes across the big boulder. Together they let out a triumphant cheer, take their first snack as a celebration of reaching their first goal, and set off with renewed vigor and confidence to conquer the climb and descent of Mount Achievement in seventeen hours. It's not record-breaking, but it's far better than average, and Team Deliberate is quite satisfied with this outcome.

Figure 9.1.

This story showcases a path to Deliberate Coaching based on the science of behavior. Let's take a look at a few critical elements by comparing and contrasting the teams.

Antecedents

In our discussion of antecedents, you learned that antecedents come before behavior to get it going. They can come in many forms, such as a comprehensive training or a simple reminder. Once outcomes have been identified, the job of a good coach is to identify the behaviors that will lead to attainment of the desired result, then see if those they are coaching possess the required skills. If they don't, the coach must make use of effective training to develop the skills. In the case of all three teams, the instructors provided instruction, modeling, and lots of rehearsal with feedback to ensure the acquisition of the critical skills. So while not all of the teams reached the top of Mount Achievement, training wasn't the issue.

Value

While we know antecedents get behavior going, it's value that keeps it going. Specifically, the value of the consequences that occur as a result of behavior.

In chapter 5 we talked about the concept of positive and negative reinforcement. Reinforcement is at the root of all performance improvement. With the exception of reflexes, all behavior occurs because antecedents start it and consequences determine whether the behavior will continue. Period. People behave to either get something or get away from something. Consider infants. Why do they cry? While initially a reflexive behavior, infants soon learn that crying sometimes results in access to something like food or warmth. Crying is positively reinforced by access to something preferred and, because of this positive reinforcement, the behavior will increase. In other cases, infants learn that crying gets them away from something like a dirty diaper or a loud noise. In this case, the behavior will increase because of negative reinforcement, where crying works to avoid or remove something unwanted.

As adults, we learn certain series or chains of behaviors can lead to some sort of meaningful outcome. Inserting a car key, pressing the brake, and turning the key are steps that will lead to the car starting and your being able to start toward your destination. But the meaningful outcome isn't always provided by the external environment, like the start of the car or feedback by a manager. The added thing can simply be feeling good about the results. A teacher who takes pride in the success of her students is one example. If she attributes some of their success to a certain instructional strategy and this increases her use of the strategy, we can now say that her behavior (using the instructional strategy) has been positively reinforced by naturally occurring positive reinforcement. Nobody had to give her praise, a gift card, or a teacher of the month award. Many teachers teach for the love of helping students. When they see students doing well, this is powerful positive reinforcement.

Now let's get back to our story. If we look at Team Chill, it's clear that climbing Mount Achievement had little value to them. It wasn't a meaningful consequence.

Instead, their behavior was impacted by the use of negative reinforcement—they climbed just far enough to get out of sight, avoiding embarrassment and perhaps the ire of their instructors and fellow group members, then headed back to the comfort of the resort. Remember, this is one of the problems with using negative reinforcement (fear of consequences) to motivate behavior. People will do just enough to get by, and typically only in the presence of the folks who can deliver the undesirable consequence. If people don't value the outcome, they're far less likely to put forth effort toward achieving it.

In the cases of Team Quick and Team Deliberate, it's clear that they both valued climbing to the top of Mount Achievement. Nobody had to look over their shoulder to make them climb. All the behaviors that brought them closer to the top were under contingencies of positive reinforcement. Recall that when people behave in ways that lead them toward what they value, they will continue behaving in those ways, even when nobody is looking.

Precise and Purposeful Planning

While both Team Quick and Team Deliberate valued reaching the top of Mount Achievement, it was precise and purposeful planning that made the difference in their speed. Team Deliberate knew precisely how far they would go based on hikers' average time. Moreover, they knew precisely what they would see when they got there. Had they not found landmarks as measurable indicators that they were moving in the right direction, the group might have gotten disheartened and returned to the base of the mountain, or even to camp, having failed to reach the top. But they didn't leave their journey to chance. They set goals based on the available data, monitored their progress based on the achievement of those goals, and celebrated short-term successes along the way.

Your personal journey applying Deliberate Coaching is much like the climb up Mount Achievement. Much like Team Deliberate, you are journeying down a path laden with reinforcement, support, and behavioral principles to accelerate your journey, and the journey of others. There are a lot of moving parts needed to achieve your goals and those of the educators you support. And a successful journey requires collaboration between you and your team of educators and staff. Your school and the interconnected systems must work in harmony to accelerate performance and maximize achievement.

Integration in a Leadership System

There is a subtle simplicity to behavior analysis. Generally speaking, as we've said before, if you see behavior, somewhere in the environment there is at least one antecedent getting that behavior going and at least one consequence responsible for keeping it going. Finding and utilizing these antecedents and consequences, particularly as part of your Deliberate Coaching system, is the cornerstone of leadership. Although our assessments and interventions might sometimes prioritize one or the other, it's important that our targeted improvement efforts involve ample amounts of both. As we've hopefully taught you, if all you do is use antecedents like training, job aids, or prompts without consequences, all you'll do is get behavior started. It won't continue unless something good happens as a result of that behavior. Conversely, if you only focus on consequences, you might be waiting a long time for the behavior to occur. You do need antecedents to nudge behavior in the right direction.

You need to understand the components of your leadership system in order to ensure that each system is functioning properly and that you have alignment across all of your systems (e.g., human resources, guidance counseling, psychology, administration). The science of behavior is involved before you hire teachers, during the hiring process, during your training and professional development, and through your coaching. Your hiring process involves putting out the expectations for the job and trying to identify behaviors of applicants, most likely indirectly through interviews, that match your expectations. Your assessment of how the repertoire of a given applicant matches the expectations and school culture will help guide your decision-making as a hirer. The training system you use for new hires or professional development will involve a series of antecedents and consequences to build the behaviors targeted by the training. Coaching takes what your teachers learn to another level.

Systems Alignment

Your school leadership system contains all of the systems that all school personnel use to get optimal results. It's important that these systems work together, with each one supporting the others, aligned and interlocked. Each system should also be evaluated as its own entity with its own goals, outcomes, and processes. Ambiguity in your systems can lead to confusion and cause one system to be overlooked, ignored because you might think that another system is meeting those needs.

For example, let's look again at behavioral skills training (BST), the well-researched training model in the behavioral literature (Johnson et al., 2005) that we spoke of in chapter 6. As a system for developing skills, the BST approach consists of providing instruction to a person on the target task being trained, having a trainer model the task, and allowing practice opportunities where the trainee can rehearse the skill and receive feedback.

As a training system, BST is an antecedent designed to help a person acquire the skill. But those skills need support in the post-training environment (for instance, the classroom) if they're to continue. A teacher needs to see that what they just learned actually works. This is where your coaching system presumably kicks in. However, a number of coaching interventions in the research literature that are labeled as coaching contain core features of training—namely instruction, modeling, and feedback (e.g., Komaki & Barnett, 1977; Shapiro & Shapiro, 1985). Do these components mean you actually have a training system rather than a coaching system?

Consider this example. A school consultant walks into a school and asks to learn about that school's coaching system, performance management system, teaching evaluation system, or any other system that might help provide day-to-day teacher support. The principal shows the consultant how her staff provides instruction to the teachers when they need help and how they model the correct way to do things and provide feedback when the teacher practices doing it. In other words, the principal describes behavioral skills training. But training is for skill deficits; what system is in place for performance problems that aren't due to skill deficits? You can't fix broken equipment or a procedural issue or a lack of reinforcement with more training. What the consultant wants to know is how the principal helps transfer and maintain skills a teacher learned in college or in a professional-development event. What the principal gave the consultant had more to do with the ways she provides training.

The applied research literature is supposed to provide scientific support and a level of clarification on the form of a strategy (what it looks like) and function (why it's used). While the science of behavior can be a valuable addition to your school leadership infrastructure, behavior coaching has been loosely defined over the years, making it difficult to disseminate proven coaching technologies (Seniuk, Witts, Williams, & Ghezzi, 2013). If you simply identify a system as "coaching" whenever it contains certain behavioral components, then you might be spending a lot of time trying to fix coaching problems with training solutions. The form might look similar because you use the same laws of behavior to build skills in a training environment as you would to refine and maintain skills in the classroom. But the purpose of training is different from the purpose of coaching. While cars and trains are subject to the same laws of physics, you wouldn't expect a conductor to show you his Ford Mustang when you ask about how the Amtrak is running.

Skill deficits should be addressed by a school's professional development and training systems. Transferring those skills and supporting day-to-day teacher performance should be addressed by your coaching system. Systems fixes should be fixed by your administrative systems. While these systems all work together, they serve different purposes. School leaders should know how each system is working and where there are opportunities to improve. If you confuse one system for another, you could be ignoring a critical piece of your school's infrastructure. Training on the effective use of a SMART Board won't do anything if the SMART Board is broken.

There are three main categories of leadership systems related to coaching and performance-improvement efforts.

Administration

A good coach takes time to observe what's going on, monitoring progress and finding ways to set a coachee up for success. Sometimes the result of an assessment or observation is that a new policy needs to be written for a school or classroom. Maybe you need to order new equipment, build a new checklist to help teachers organize a new activity, or tweak a couple items in the academic calendar of events. All of these are things you've identified as barriers hindering teacher performance. They're all important duties of a good leader, even if they aren't part of your coaching.

Training

Professional development, continued education, modeling, and other forms of training are critical to ensuring that teachers know what to do. But let's be clear that it's not the *knowing* that dictates the success of training—it's whether a teacher can demonstrate the trained skills at a high enough level that you can reasonably expect them to use them in the classroom.

Regardless of how good your training is (how much *demonstrable* learning it produces), it's still just an antecedent. It will still only get behavior going. You need to provide opportunities to practice these skills in the classroom, and once teachers try them out, good things have to result or they won't use them anymore.

Coaching

Training and administration have stopping points. Remember, the demonstration of learning is the main goal of training (Johnson & Rubin, 2011; Molenda & Russell, 2006). Someone has a skill deficit, needs training, gets trained, training ends, and the person is presumably good to go. A process needs to be fixed, someone fixes it, the new process gets rolled out, and the new process is in effect. Coaching doesn't stop. Coaching, in particular the type of *behavioral* coaching described here, involves the ongoing use of behavioral strategies to directly impact performance (Weatherly, in review). Coaching helps facilitate the transfer of skills trained into the workplace environment.

Deliberate Coaching Defined

If the school were a movie set, teachers would deserve the leading role. Since good instruction has the largest impact on student achievement, every other adult in the building should be thought of as a supporting cast member, putting teachers in a position where they can shine like the stars the students need them to be. In much of the recent educational literature there is a call for school leaders to help teachers excel by not only focusing on the managerial demands of school leadership, but to also focus on the specific tasks required for improving classroom instruction (Steiner & Kowal, 2007).

Some school leaders attempt to spread out their leadership responsibilities by delegating leadership duties across personnel. Some leaders seek to embed a coaching program into their school by employing classroom-level instructional coaches who provide teachers with needed support (Spillane, Halverson, & Diamond, 2001). However, it's not as simple as just hiring instructional coaches and hoping for the best.

For a coaching program to be effective, school leaders must develop a coaching strategy as part of their school improvement plan, select the right coaches, evaluate the impact of coaching, and provide regular feedback to encourage and guide coaching efforts. Essentially, the school leader must act as a coach to the coaches.

Deliberate Coaching

As we've discussed, deliberate practice refers to practice that is purposeful and systematic. While regular practice might include mindless repetitions, deliberate practice requires focused attention and is conducted with the specific goal of improving performance.

"Good leaders are like good coaches. They know how to bring out the best in people on their team."
—John Maxwell

Borrowing from this familiar concept, we describe Deliberate Coaching as coaching that goes beyond the functional definition we've previously outlined.

Deliberate Coaching is a model of behavioral coaching that revolves around precise, purposeful, and systematic coaching interactions. Deliberate Coaching is implemented by internal personnel to directly impact workplace behaviors that are aligned with workplace results. As an approach that's based in research on the science of behavior, Deliberate Coaching requires focused observation, tracking of performance change, and feedback to shape socially valid, high-impact behavior. And when we say socially valid, we mean behaviors that are acceptable to both the people implementing a particular coaching intervention (e.g., the teacher) and those receiving the intervention (e.g., the students). Let's take a look at the principles used to guide Deliberate Coaching:

Precise

- Measurement of performance that is specific, detailed, and frequent
- Clear distinction between the development of skills (training) and transference of skills
- Feedback that is specific to a pinpointed behavior
- Feedback that links behavior to pinpointed results

Purposeful

- Linked to on-the-job outcome
- Intentionally designed with positive procedures
- Sustained focus on a few pinpointed behaviors

Systematic

- Uses specific behavioral procedures that have been experimentally demonstrated to be effective and are repeatable
- Measures improvement against a performer's own performance
- Uses measurement of performance to guide coaching behavior
- Uses social validity to monitor and guide coaching interventions

The Deliberate Coaching process is designed to work within the constraints of any environment. Each school has unique parameters that need to be acknowledged and respected. Precision allows for objectivity, taking away subjective judgement that can cloud progress and moving toward focused directives. Purposeful coaching ensures there is a reason behind the coaching that both the coach and the coachee can see. Being systematic ensures you're taking things in manageable increments, monitoring your progress, and ensuring efforts are supported and goals are reasonable. These foundational targets can set up any coach for success!

CHAPTER 10

THE 8 Ws OF DELIBERATE COACHING

Don't just teach your kids to read. Teach them to question what they read. Teach them to question everything.

—George Carlin

Famed leadership guru John Maxwell recognized questioning as foundational to successful leadership. In his book *Good Leaders Ask Great Questions* (2014), Maxwell notes, "If you want to be successful and reach your leadership potential, you need to embrace asking questions as a lifestyle" (p. 4). And we can say the same about Deliberate Coaching. While high levels of practice and feedback typically occur in the early stages of effective skill development, Deliberate Coaches understand that to support the transference of those skills into the natural environment, they should progressively fade from *telling* to *questioning.*

Having a good "ask" through coaching questions is an effective method for engaging the teacher in their own performance improvement. Questioning allows the teacher to reflect on the link between their behavior and outcomes; moreover, it creates many more opportunities for the coach to gather information that can be used to guide coaching interactions.

Raising good questions is not new to educators. An art that requires cultivated and practiced knowledge (Cavanaugh & Warwick, 2001), it is fundamental to stimulating student thinking (Aschner, 1961). Posing questions pertinent to a specific scope of knowledge will facilitate the learning process. In the field of language learning and teaching, the importance of questioning as a teaching and learning strategy is well documented (Almeida, 2010; Chin & Osborne, 2008; Graesser & Olde, 2003;

Chin, 2007; Roth, 1996). Students' level of engagement largely depends on the questions formulated by the teachers in the classroom that prompt and guide thinking (Wilen, 1991) and on the questions generated by students themselves in the process of learning and teaching (Almeida, 2010, 2012).

This concept applies to adults as well as many coaching experts (e.g., Knight, 2009; Maxwell, 2014; Souza, 2015; Wilson, 2007) advocate questioning be used to allow the coachee to reflect on their practice. This also allows both the coach and coachee to collaboratively gain new insights and better inform future practice. Indeed, there is a developing focus among researchers on questioning strategies as they're an indispensable element in developing, expanding, and challenging thinking (Klem & Connell, 2004; Marzano, Pickering, & Pollock, 2001; Miciano, 2004).

Questioning to Avoid Prompt Dependency

Say it's late in the afternoon and you are making the drive to see your friend an hour north. Though you've visited him many times over the past year since he's moved to the area, you plug his address into the GPS like you always do so you can put your mind, along with the car, on cruise control. You sit back, turn the radio on, and sing along to kill time.

About fifty minutes into the drive, the unthinkable happens. After going haywire for a moment, the GPS shuts down, never to grace the interior of your car with its colorful screen again. Before you have a chance to mourn the death of your former electronic companion, you realize that you have no idea where you are! Though you've made the trip dozens of times, your now defunct electronic buddy has always guided your every move. As a result, you don't recognize the landmarks or even the exit where you normally get off, as they all look similar.

In the story above, you've become a victim to the phenomenon known as *prompt dependency* (Cooper, Heron, & Heward, 2007). In short, prompt dependency occurs when somebody regularly needs prompting in the form of instruction, explanations, illustrations, or even gestures to complete a task. Prompting in and of itself isn't a bad thing—it's actually critical to teaching and learning during early stages of skill acquisition. However, when people are always told what to do during training or coaching as opposed to responding to natural cues, they tend to become dependent on the trainer or coach. This is likely because they haven't had to exercise important skills like discriminating, problem solving, or decision-making to accomplish the task.

To avoid prompt dependency, behavior science recommends a powerful yet simple procedure: *fading*. Fading occurs when prompts are systematically reduced. While the term might seem foreign, you've done it and had it done to you often throughout your life. For example, before you learned to walk independently, your parent might have first held both hands, then one hand, and then let you hold a finger. This systematic fading of physical guidance occurred until you acquired the correct balance and movement and no longer needed the additional help. The same thing occurred when you learned to discriminate between colors. Your mom might have said to you, "That's reeeeeddddd. What color is it?" And you responded, "Red!" After some repetition, you were eventually able to respond correctly, without the precorrection. Your mom simply used a question—"What color is it?"—to evoke the appropriate response, "Red!" While this kind of questioning is commonly used on children, many adults don't understand how powerful it actually is.

The 8 Ws of Deliberate Coaching

Since we don't want teachers to always rely on coaches telling them what to do and why it's important, what kinds of questions should be asked? There are actually quite a few books dedicated to this very subject. However, Deliberate Coaching is primarily concerned with two things: behavior and results. The function of questioning, therefore, should be to help the educator recognize the impact of their behavior on the desired result and to provide the coach an opportunity to assess and give feedback. As such, we recommend that Deliberate Coaches seek precise behavioral responses that get educators to self-identify:

1. their own behavior (good and bad)
2. the results of their behavior
3. why the behavior is occurring
4. what to do instead
5. why the behavior is important (particularly in terms of the impact on consequences that matter to them personally)

Good coaches ask great questions to get educators in touch with naturally occurring positive reinforcement. They do this by helping them to look for even the smallest positive changes in their environment that result from their behavior. When this happens, educators will continue attempting a task, skill, or process, even in the absence of the coach.

The five Ws (who, what, where, when, why) are often referenced as a problem-solving guide, originating in concept with ancient philosophers like Aristotle and evolving over time in applications of science and information gathering (Sloan, 2010). The Deliberate Coaching process is a science-based process that shares a similar need for information gathering and problem solving. The process must be tracked and built upon to ensure that coaches are making a significant impact. The 8 Ws of Deliberate Coaching capture this process and function as both a guide for planning and a way to report how your coaching interactions went.

8 Ws of Deliberate Coaching	
Who? Who are you coaching?	
Which? Which behaviors are linked to which goals/results?	
Why? Why are you choosing a particular coaching task?	
When? When will you coach?	
Where? Where are you coaching?	
What? What will/did you do?	
What Happened? What was the impact?	
Why Don't . . . ? What will you do next?	

Figure 10.1.

Who?

Who are you coaching? Although there is a time and place for group discussions, coaching interactions are a one-on-one exchange. What's reinforcing for one person might not be reinforcing for another person, and what's causing a performance problem for one person might be completely different for someone else. Because of this, you should make plans for and report on one person at a time.

Example. Put yourself in the position of a vice principal responsible for a team of teachers. You will need to identify one teacher per 8-Ws form. The goal of this form is to plan, track, review, and systematically move forward with an individualized approach to teacher support.

Which?

Out of all the results your direct reports are responsible for, which one are you targeting? Out of all the behaviors that lead to those results, which behaviors are you targeting? There must be alignment between behavior and results, and coaches must monitor both to make sure you're getting change and getting it the right way. And these pinpoints need to be clear to all applicable parties. The objectivity of your pinpoints is essential to ensuring that you know what you're focusing on, you know what to track and how to discuss progress, and you can provide a level of clarity during feedback discussions. This is the information that needs to be provided to your coachees while you're tracking where they've been and where they're going. Remaining transparent and clear along this journey will help you gain credibility as a coach. You want them to trust you. You want them to *want* to be coached. You need to justify to yourself, your teacher, and your supervisors why you selected the behaviors you're coaching. Your time is valuable, and what you do with that time is important.

Example. Ms. Reid is a new teacher, and her students have been scoring low on their math tests recently. Math is an important area in subsequent grades and in school standardized assessments, so it's imperative that these scores come up. While observing and discussing this with Ms. Reid and exemplar teachers, it becomes apparent that she runs through her fluency flashcards slowly, losing her students' attention in the process. Getting her to increase attention by using the flashcards quickly should help improve her students' scores.

Why?

Why are you coaching? In particular, why are you planning to coach in a specific way? Everything in Deliberate Coaching is linked to the coaching interaction, but coaching behaviors can extend beyond it.

Example. You've already observed to locate the target behavior, target results, and current levels of performance. And you've already worked with Ms. Reid to find out why she's been struggling with her speed. She hadn't realized that her students, not attending to her during the activity was such a critical piece of the puzzle. She was able to verbally demonstrate how to get her students to attend, so the next step is to provide support by intervening with a coaching interaction to get her to actually apply this knowledge.

When?

When is the best time for your coaching? When does the behavior occur most frequently? When are there opportunities for the behavior to occur? Most likely your school won't have a staff of free-roaming coaches, meaning that only a limited number of school leaders will be functioning as coaches. Your school will need to allocate coaching wisely if each teacher is to get the support they need. One way to do this is carefully planning when you're going to observe, when you're going to assess, and when you're going to have your quick coaching interactions.

Example. Ms. Reid's math activities occur at 10:30 a.m. and 2:00 p.m. The best time to offer support would be during or immediately after these activities. You don't want to interrupt the lessons, but if you observe and then provide feedback directly once school ends, this should allow you to gather the information you need for your feedback and give Ms. Reid the privacy she needs when you discuss her performance.

Where?

Where will the coaching take place? This is directly linked to the "when" component in that you're trying to maximize the time you're spending on coaching in an agreed-upon area that is conducive to coaching interactions.

Example. Seeing as the coaching interaction will come after the students have left, it will take place in Ms. Reid's classroom.

What?

Based on what you know about a particular educator's performance, what do you need to do as a coach to move forward? What are you *planning* to do? Afterwards, what did you *actually* do? (Hopefully it's the same as what you planned, but sometimes things come up.) Here are some potential things a coach might do, all of which are part of or at least linked to the coaching interaction.

Observation

In order to coach, you need to know what's happening with the person you're coaching. You can't coach without pinpointing behaviors and results, and you can't coach without understanding what's going on around the behavior. To find these things, you need to look around and observe what occurs before, during, and after the behavior. If you're trying to help a teacher improve student participation, for instance, it's good to see what the teacher is currently doing to get that participation and what conditions are surrounding these behaviors. When planning your coaching, sometimes the coaching behavior you're focusing on for a given day is focused on assessment by observing to find the "which" and the "what."

Assessment

Deliberate coaching is purposeful coaching. Your coaching interactions must serve a purpose, and this purpose should not be a guess. An efficient coach maximizes the coaching interaction by using behavior science to assess why bad things are happening and why good things are happening. (Don't make the mistake of ignoring the good things or they might go away!) Using tools like the Performance Diagnostic Checklist to assess why behavior problems are occurring and identifying antecedents and consequences surrounding desired and undesired teacher performance will help you find the right coaching solution for the situation. You don't want to recommend training if it's not a training problem, and you don't want to waste time with constructive feedback if the problem is a bad process or faulty equipment. Trial and error is costly and time-consuming, so sometimes the best thing for a coach to do is assess. Then you can use the information you gather to guide the coaching interaction.

Prompting

Behavior needs something to get it going. Optimally these antecedents occur naturally in the environment so that a teacher is simply reacting to normal classroom events. The time of day prompts the teacher that a new activity should begin. A student's question prompts the teacher to address that student's need. If a particular student has been struggling with multiplication, then a new multiplication activity should prompt the teacher to check on that student. But sometimes people need a nudge. Your coaching interaction could offer some quick and well-timed advice, asking the teacher to discuss the safety procedures prior to leaving on a field trip or reminding the teacher about what seemed to work the last time during a particular activity. You know that the teacher *can* do the skill, but sometimes a prompt is the type of antecedent they need to get things going.

Feedback

Feedback is information about what the person is doing, targeted at improving performance. It can be positive, highlighting what someone is doing well and why it's important, or it can be constructive, identifying what the person did wrong, what should be done instead, and why this change is important. Each type of feedback can be used by a coach as both an antecedent to get behavior going or as a consequence, depending on how and when it's delivered. Say that a teacher has typically struggled to maintain order when her class is walking to lunch. If you provide the teacher feedback *before* lunch, the feedback is an antecedent. Your intent is to guide her upcoming transition. If you provide the teacher feedback *after* lunch, the feedback becomes a consequence, helping to maintain the teacher performance. In this case, the feedback could actually be working as a *dual-functioning chained stimulus* in that it serves two purposes: to reinforce the response that came before it (what the teacher did correctly during the transition to lunch) and prompt the response that comes next (what the teacher does during the transition from lunch to the classroom).

This is a good way to use constructive feedback, as it's critical to provide positive feedback once the teacher engages in the new preferred behavior. This shows the teacher that you're paying attention when good things happen too, and you don't just pop in for the bad things. It helps build trust, showing that if you say you'll follow up, you actually do follow up. And it gives you the opportunity to show that there is value in doing things the preferred way, both in terms of how it impacts the teacher's work and in terms of the positive reinforcement you offer as a coach.

In order to provide feedback in the kind of specific and individualized way that makes it effective, you need to know what results and behaviors you're targeting, why the performance is where it is, when the best time is to offer feedback, and the other items in the 8 Ws. You might be able to find some of this information by asking good questions during the coaching interaction. If not, that's where the observation and assessment come in. Although performance feedback is a critical piece of the coaching interaction, don't neglect the observation and assessment that help maximize the impact of your feedback.

Bruce Tulgan's FAST Feedback approach (1999) offers a useful toolbox to guide feedback interactions. The approach, consistent with the standards of behavior analysis offered in the Deliberate Coaching process, maintains a focus on individualization and consistency.

- *Frequent.* Feedback needs to occur frequently enough to shape behavior and provide follow-up for corrected performance.
- *Accurate.* There is a level of trust between a coach and the person being coached. This trust is built in part through establishing clear pinpoints and providing accurate feedback related to them. Without it accuracy in feedback, the coachee and the coach won't be on the same page. Imagine you're a teacher, and your principal comes in to give you feedback on the low scores in your classroom. But the data she's reporting to you are wrong—they're from a different classroom. This error won't exactly build confidence in the feedback to follow! Accuracy helps build trust because it feels good to know with reliability that you and the coach are talking about the same thing.
- *Specific.* It's possible to be specific about a behavior and a result, but not accurate. It's critical to have both accuracy and specificity, and for similar reasons. You and the person you're providing feedback to need to agree on what you're talking about. Vague feedback like "You did a good job today" or "Try to fix the quality of your lesson plan" won't get you anywhere. What you mean by quality and what the teacher means by quality are most likely completely different.
- *Timely.* As we've discussed before, the closer the consequence is to the behavior, the more impactful the consequence will be. If your feedback is frequent, then it should also be timely.

Example. When coaching Ms. Reid, the goal is to provide a quick interaction that won't keep her from her afterschool duties but allows ample time to note her past performance, note her current progress, and ask questions about what she feels is working and what she feels is not.

And that's essentially what you ended up doing. You were able to observe and provide feedback without delay once the students were out of the classroom. You provided a positive feedback statement that was specific to her improvements in getting the students to attend, and you discussed the value of this improvement in her day, the ease of the activity given these improvements, and the impact on student outcomes.

What Happened?

After you provided the coaching interaction, what happened? Has the behavior changed? Has there been any change in results yet? What did the person do while you were coaching them? The goal is to get results, but get results in the right way to build a positive school culture. This means that you need to monitor results, monitor the behaviors of the teacher that lead to those results, and monitor the body language and interaction the teacher has as you're coaching them. If you're getting results and behavior change, but the teacher is avoiding eye contact with you or deflecting blame (or credit) to others during constructive and positive feedback conversations, this could be an indicator that the teacher doesn't like your coaching interactions. This could lead to the teacher doing just enough to avoid having those coaching interactions with you, which is not good. You want a teacher to not only see value in your coaching, but see so much value that they actually start approaching you to talk about their performance because good things happen when they do.

Example. Ms. Reid initially seemed uncomfortable with your observations. She's not used to being regularly tracked, and historically, tracking performance meant she'd only hear from her supervisor when something was wrong. But now she seems eager to discuss her progress after class. She smiles and actually approaches you in the hallway before you even get to her classroom to tell you about the progress she's made. And it seems to be working so far. Student test scores are increasing, and it appears that almost all students are attending prior to the math lessons.

Why Don't ...?

"Why don't you try the changes we discussed during your next class, and I'll check back to see how things went?" "Why don't you send me an email once the changes are made to your curriculum and let me know if there's anything I can do to help." The Deliberate Coaching process doesn't stop because teacher performance doesn't stop. Shaping behavior into long-lasting habits takes time. Educators always need to be recognized for the good work they're doing and need support to help them make tweaks here and there to maximize performance.

Example. Ms. Reid is making real progress, so your next steps are to continue to reinforce her progress and emphasize how her improvements are impacting her day-to-day work and student outcomes. Asking questions like "How is this making your day better?" could get her talking about natural reinforcers!

The 8-Ws form should be one of the first tools you use, as it's designed to both prompt your coaching behaviors and track progress. When coaching coaches to use this form, remember that, as with any new behavior, you want to reinforce its use, so start small. First, simply reinforce bringing the form and filling it out, in whatever way the coach likes. Then you can start shaping up the quality and constancy of the information in the form. But using it is imperative. If they don't, they'll be leading without any order or structure.

Planning, Tracking, and Follow-Up

Remember that Deliberate Coaching is an ongoing process. The 8 Ws of Deliberate Coaching are designed to keep you focused on a precise target based on the needs of the educator being coached. Following these eight areas allows you to plan your coaching, track how things are going, and use this information to keep the progress coming strategically and steadily. The clarity of how you communicate about your coaching is critical, both for personal growth as a leader and for transparency with those you're working for and with. Your goal is to make the coaching process valuable to your direct reports by helping them with things that matter. You do this by being precise, purposeful, and systematic. And you build a positive school culture by keeping this going so that you and the other coaches make the lives of all educators and staff members better through your support. In turn, they will make the lives of the students better, which is our ultimate goal.

Tracking can simply mean providing a brief description of what you're seeing. You might even just create a couple of boxes (see figure 10.2) as a way to quickly note progress on your pinpoints and linked results. Keeping these together helps align the two, making sure your focus remains on both the specific teacher behavior and the reason why that behavior is important (the outcome).

<table>
<tr><th>Teacher Behavior(s):</th><th>Student Behavior(s)/Achievement:</th></tr>
<tr><td>||||||</td><td>|||||||</td></tr>
</table>

Figure 10.2.

You might also wish to consider a more formal way of tracking teacher performance via the related results. You want your data to be as objective as possible, but we understand that measurement can be time-consuming. So do what you can, but the more data the better! The information you gather should tell a story about how things are going. What's working and what's not working. The more precise these data are, the more buy-in you'll get. If you make subjective judgements about behavior, then you might get into a battle of what you think is going on versus what the teacher says is going on. That isn't a battle you want to be in, and there's no way for either person to win it. You can prevent this issue by getting more precise data. Cut off potential confrontations through objectivity. Try observing and counting the behaviors. Or have the teacher keep a tally. For instance, if you want to know how many times a teacher asked for engagement during a lesson, try to tally this up. If you want to know how many of those answers were correct, mark it and tally a percentage. You can create a simple form like the boxes above to keep track of your tallies, and something like the simple graph options depicted below as a coaching tool to help you and your coachee observe trends.

Individual versus Organizational Coaching

To be successful in their endeavors, it is our belief that school leaders should be provided regular learning opportunities that focus on more than just individualized instructional practice and management strategies. They must be coached in organizational leadership strategies and the effective use of measurement and feedback to *positively* impact student achievement on a larger scale.

For the last decade or so, we've read a ton of educational literature touting the need for principals to be "instructional leaders" who make suggestions, provide feedback, model effective instruction, solicit opinions, support collaboration, arrange learning opportunities for teachers, and provide regular praise for effective teaching (Blasé & Blasé, 2000). Moreover, instructional leaders are called on to "work closely with students, developing teaching techniques and methods as a means for understanding teacher perspectives and for establishing a base on which to make curricular decisions" (Jenkins, 2009).

All of this sounds super. So much so that district and school leaders frequently view instructional leadership as the Holy Grail of student achievement and pour a ton of resources into developing their declarative (understanding "what to do") knowledge regarding instructional practices that will maximize student performance. And this makes sense since good instruction leads to student achievement. As we mentioned, teachers must be the stars of the show, and school leadership should seek to make them shine. Still, there's a fly in the ointment. A major assumption of this approach is that all school leaders are in a position to directly influence teaching through individualized coaching practices such as modeling and direct feedback. Given the demands of school leaders, it's safe to say that too often they're not in a position to provide this type of coaching. This is especially true in schools that support economically disadvantaged students. Don't take our word for it, just ask them!

As leaders and coaches, we are clearly huge supporters of a little instruction and modeling coupled with a *lot* of helpful feedback that's presented in a way that encourages growth. But sometimes individual coaching yields little return on investment, especially when a lot of attention, feedback, and support are needed across a struggling school and there is little to give because of competing demands. Telling school leaders of struggling schools to focus more on instruction and less on management and operations doesn't work when these areas aren't functioning effectively. Can you imagine a principal in a school that was struggling with misbehavior providing individualized coaching to a teacher when basic processes like schoolwide routines and procedures weren't in place for behavior management? It would likely be chaos. And while the one teacher might benefit in the moment, all of the students and teachers as a whole would be negatively impacted as a result of failure to develop, train, and coach students and staff in systems required to create a positive and safe climate and culture.

We obviously do believe in individual coaching at the classroom level, and we will continue to provide you with tools for accelerating teacher performance in the remainder of this book. With its focus on a teacher's classroom instruction, it's clearly extremely effective under the right conditions. In moderate- to high-achieving schools, there tends to be a positive climate and culture of learning that reduces the frequency of problematic issues inherent to struggling schools. In schools where most teachers are reaching at least a moderate level of success, good coaching interventions at the individual level are likely to have the desired outcome.

However, if you've ever been in a failing school, you know very well that school leaders are frequently mired in issues that prevent them from entering the classroom often enough to directly impact instruction through direct coaching. In addition, members of their leadership or coaching team who are tasked with further developing the teachers' instructional behaviors are often met with a litany of similar roadblocks. Unfortunately, unhappy parents, misbehaving students, and disgruntled staff commonly plague the hallways and classrooms of these schools.

To exacerbate the problem, if you look at the organizational structure of some schools, you will note that the staff-to-administrator ratio is far from that recommended by many researchers. Again, in the right environment, this ratio can be adequate, but these conditions are commonly absent in schools that are in need of transformation.

For leaders charged with initiating large-scale change like turning around a struggling school, we believe the emphasis should initially be on Deliberate Coaching at the organizational level, *not* at the individual level where there is a narrow focus on individual instructional practices. Don't get us wrong. Teachers obviously need to possess good knowledge of instructional practices. The problem is, this focus alone is insufficient for success in struggling schools.

Where individual coaching tends to be focused on day-to-day instructional practices, organizational coaching focuses on getting the right people in the right place, then systematically and collectively building the skill *and* will of all staff in the school setting and doing so in a way that will positively impact school culture and classroom instruction. Where individual coaches focus on the individual as the unit of analysis, the organizational coach focuses on the group as a whole by:

- Simplifying and placing focus on a few key expectations at a time
- Positively influencing all teachers and staff
- Setting high expectations for student achievement across the campus
- Standardizing and streamlining schoolwide processes and procedures
- Engaging all teachers and staff by involving them in regular data analysis, goal development, and action planning at the organizational level

Organizational coaching strategies help improve teacher performance by improving systems and processes to achieve collective student success. For the purpose of this book, organizational coaching is a *very specific skill set* rooted in organizational behavior management (OBM). Organizational coaches possess the skill sets of the individual coach. Like individual coaches, they do recognize that teacher instruction has the biggest impact on student achievement. However, where instructional coaches are highly knowledgeable in instructional practices and skilled at providing direct coaching in the classroom, organizational coaches are also skilled at systematically supporting the progressive growth of all staff. They focus on engaging and retaining effective teachers by developing larger systemic approaches to support effective instructional practices, allowing them to bring out the best in students.

For example, an organizational coach might seek to build and retain quality teachers by improving induction processes that promote career learning, provide multiple personnel with access to support, and treat induction as part of a lifelong professional development design (Breaux & Wong, 2003).

After collaboratively developing key systems based on comprehensive assessments, organizational coaches identify a few key behaviors (as opposed to trying to tackle many), then focus on systematically developing performance in a way that turns staff who don't help into staff who want to help. These leaders understand how to leverage measurement through leading and lagging indicators (more on these later) to assess, support, and celebrate progressive movement toward goals.

Just as the measure of a teacher is in the learner, the measure of a coach can be found in those they're coaching. The greatest coaches help turn coachees into coaches. While every coach can't be the greatest (by definition there is only one), every coach can increase student achievement by understanding how to deliberately influence individual *and* collective performance of their students, faculty, and staff.

If you are effectively using individual coaching to support instructional improvement at your school, keep doing it! In small schools with a good culture, individual coaching is a great approach, especially when tempered with supportive leadership. But please keep reading so you can continue deepening your Deliberate Coaching toolbox to also positively impact groups of people utilizing the same scientific principles.

If individual coaching isn't working, try taking a step back and looking at developing systems that foster large-scale instructional improvement. Perhaps the right approach is organizational coaching. But whichever approach you use, remember this: if students are going to reach their greatest potential, all school leaders must move beyond management that's characterized by holding people accountable. The best Deliberate Coaches, whether using an individual or organizational approach, remain *precise, purposeful, and systematic.* They understand the importance of the 8 Ws across all of their coaching interactions, and they regularly apply the most powerful tool available for creating a sustainable culture of achievement: positive reinforcement.

CHAPTER 11

PRECISE COACHING

It is the mark of an educated mind to rest satisfied with the degree of precision which the nature of the subject admits and not to seek exactness where only an approximation is possible.

—Aristotle

In performance improvement, pinpointing is the process of describing precisely what outcome is desired and precisely what behavior should occur to achieve the outcome (Daniels & Daniels, 2006). It may sound oversimplistic, but failure to accurately pinpoint both the outcome *and* behavior is responsible for many of the performance issues that exist in organizations. Remember, all results require somebody doing something more, less, or differently. A focus on outcome data alone (e.g., student achievement) disregards the actual behavior required to achieve desired results.

As you know, one of the guiding principles of Deliberate Coaching is precision. And precision is at the root of pinpointing. It first requires a careful analysis of the desired results as well as the behaviors required to achieve that outcome. Not just any results or behaviors, mind you, but *precise* results and specific, observable behaviors. Simply put, you're asking where we want to go and how we want to get there. But be careful, sometimes it's not as easy as it sounds.

Imagine vacationing in Orlando with your family. While eating dinner one evening, you overhear a couple talking about their trip to a beautiful secluded beach in Florida. It sounds like an amazing place, so you lean over, apologize for eavesdropping, and politely ask where the beach is. The couple laughs. They share a few more tantalizing facts about the beach and tourist attractions in the surrounding area, then give you the name of the town. "A trip to Four Candles would be a great experience for any family," they say.

The next morning, you excitedly pack your bags, load up the rented minivan, and fumble with the rental's GPS until you're able to enter Four Candles as a destination. After three hours of traveling east, following the precise directions provided by the GPS, you arrive at Four Candles. While the town appears to be pleasant enough, it isn't at all what was described by the couple. In fact, when you make your way to the beach, you're surprised to find it isn't secluded at all, but rather overcrowded.

Confused, you park the car and walk up to the local lifeguard to inquire about the secluded beach you heard about. The lifeguard chuckles. "This is the only beach in Four Candles, and it's always packed!"

"Where's the Four Candles trolley tour we heard about?"

"Trolley tour?" the lifeguard repeats, confused.

"Yes, we were told by a nice couple in Orlando that Four Candles had a secluded beach and a town with quite a few tourist attractions."

The lifeguard takes this in. "I think I know what happened. You've confused Four Candles with Fork Handles, which is a town with tourist attractions and a secluded beach. The only problem is, it's about five hours away, on the *west coast* of Florida."

Though you followed all of the GPS's directions precisely, you didn't achieve the desired outcome because the destination and the precise behaviors or "path" to get there wasn't pinpointed. Similarly, while the ultimate destination in education is student achievement, you must take care to identify long- *and* short-term goals that will provide a clear path that will eventually lead to desired growth. This requires precise and purposeful planning—you must figure out exactly which behaviors and goals will eventually lead to the kind of achievement you desire.

As a coach, determining the exact result is critical. It's not unusual for folks to jump right in with the good intention of helping a teacher in need. If you ever feel like doing this, remember the story above. If you'd done a little research on the internet prior to getting on the road, you and your family would have reached the *correct* destination in a reasonable amount of time. If you were traveling the old-fashioned way using a paper map, you would have likely identified some destinations along the way as benchmarks to let you know you were headed in the right direction as opposed to arriving and realizing you were in the wrong spot. These initial destinations are akin to short-term goals. They aren't the desired outcome, but they're leading indicators of success that let you know you're on the right path. These leading indicators are metrics that are taken frequently enough that you can use them to continuously track how well your coaching is doing.

In a similar scenario, imagine being provided the correct destination with handwritten directions (your GPS is not working), but you fail to reach the correct location as a result of a simple mistake. Specifically, somewhere along the trip you made a right turn when you should have made a left. In this case, the pinpointed behaviors outlined in the directions (e.g., drive north there, turn left here, etc.) were off. As a result of one small error, you didn't reach your destination.

The point is that pinpointing necessitates careful thought. It's not something that should be rushed into so you can jump in and do something. It requires a clear understanding of precisely where you want to go and precisely how you are going to get there.

SMART Pinpoints

You've likely heard the acronym "SMART" described differently by a variety of authors as it relates to goals. For example, a SMART goal has been defined as one that is specific, measurable, achievable, results-focused, and timebound (Doran, 1981).

For the purpose of SMART pinpointing during Deliberate Coaching, consider the SMART acronym as it is defined by Dr. Scott Geller (2003):

- *Specific.* The result and behaviors required to achieve it are clear and observable. Focus should be on what the teacher should do as opposed to what they shouldn't. For example, if students were calling out answers instead of raising their hands, a good pinpointed result would be "Increasing hand raising to answer questions." A specific behavior for the teacher to engage in might be "Only call on students who raise their hands" as opposed to "Ignore students who call out."
- *Motivational.* Simply put, the result needs to be meaningful to the teacher, and the effort worth the result. Many results are objectively important (e.g., increased student achievement, decreased misbehavior); however, if the effort required to achieve them is too much from the teacher's perspective, this is not a SMART pinpoint. The teacher is less likely to engage in the necessary behaviors.
- *Achievable.* This might seem like a no-brainer, but a pinpoint must be achievable. If it requires complex behaviors that require days' or weeks' worth of training, then this is likely not an achievable behavioral pinpoint. And if results are achievable, but the outcome is too far down the line (e.g., half the school years is through), then this is also likely not a SMART pinpoint.
- *Relevant.* Is the pinpointed behavior related to the day-to-day activities required of a teacher, and will the outcomes be meaningful to those impacted? For example, pinpointed teaching of French in English class is likely not a relevant behavior, and will likely not be meaningful to the students who want to learn about subjects related to English!
- *Trackable.* Both the pinpointed behaviors and results should be measurable. Period. If it can't be measured, it's not a pinpoint. Stating that students will behave "better" or a teacher will "improve teaching" is neither

specific nor trackable. However, stating that students will "remain in their assigned area" or a teacher will "increase the rate of questioning" is something that can be counted. There are two ways to measure: judgement (subjective assessment) and counting (cold, hard data). When it comes to Deliberate Coaching, counting always wins the day!

Consider using the SMART Pinpoints Checklist to build this process using your own results and own behavior pinpoints. This checklist will help you walk through the process of checking off the SMART criteria while aligning results and behavior.

Teacher Name:______________________________ Date:__________________

SMART Pinpoints Checklist				
Specific	**Motivational**	**Achievable**	**Relevant**	**Trackable**
The result and behaviors required to achieve it are both clear and observable.	The result is meaningful to the teacher, and the effort worth the result.	The result is obtainable, and the teacher has the skills to reach it.	The behavior is related to daily activities and will positively impact students.	Both the pinpointed behaviors and results are measureable.

Pinpointed result

Why is the result socially valid?

Pinpointed behaviors
1. ____________________
2. ____________________
3. ____________________
4. ____________________

What leading indicators will be used to measure progress?

Equipment, process, training, or support needed to achieve this result

Figure 11.1.

Choosing the Right Pinpoints

Imagine walking into a teacher's class for the first time and encountering chaos. Some students are talking during the lesson, two students appear to be sleeping, and a couple of students have even ignored the teacher after they were asked to have a seat. So where do you start? Three concepts will enable you to determine pinpoints: quick wins, stages of concern, and behavioral cusps.

Quick Wins

If you've just begun working with a teacher, we would suggest starting with a "Quick Win" (Gavoni & Rodriguez, 2016). A quick win entails helping the teacher complete relatively easy tasks before making requests that might be more challenging; moreover, it requires pinpointing a result that will be meaningful to the teacher and make an easily observable difference. While it might not have an immediate and direct impact on the bottom line of student achievement, it's ultimately aligned with that goal (e.g., increasing on-task behavior is a prerequisite for learning).

A quick win in the example above might be collaborating with the teacher to develop a plan that addresses behavior issues during morning arrival. Depending on the need, the quick win might be something as simple as having assigned seats for students and a question written on the board as a primer for the morning lesson. If this strategy results in a visible improvement in student behavior during morning arrival, you've just achieved a quick win, and the teacher is more likely to work with you in the future.

A major benefit of choosing a quick win is that it establishes you as a reinforcer: because you helped the teacher implement a relatively simple strategy that resulted in a meaningful outcome, they'll be more likely to seek you out for assistance in the future. And as we suggested earlier, they'll also be more likely to attempt progressively more complex tasks in the future.

Stages of Concern

When pinpointing, it's critical that the teacher be involved in the process. While they may not always be aware of which behaviors lead to the results they want, they know *what* results they want. Determining which short- and long-term outcomes are important to them ensures that the pinpoints are relevant.

Research related to stages of concern supports the idea of choosing outcomes that are immediately meaningful to the teacher. Developed in the 1970s and 1980s by investigators at the University of Texas at Austin, the stages of concern are broken down into seven categories and essentially provides a framework of what's important to a teacher as they progress in learning and applying a skill or "innovation" within the classroom (George, Hall, & Stiegelbauer, 2006). According to the researchers, teachers are more likely to have self-focused concerns during early stages of change; however, as they become more proficient in their job, they begin shifting their focus to the broader impact of their performance.

IMPACT	6	Refocusing	The individual focuses on exploring ways to reap more universal benefits from the innovation, including the possibility of making major changes to it or replacing it with a more powerful alternative.
	5	Collaboration	The individual focuses on coordinating and cooperating with others regarding use of the innovation.
	4	Consequence	The individual focuses on the innovation's impact on students in his or her immediate sphere of influence. Considerations include the relevance of the innovation for students; the evaluation of student outcomes, including performance and competencies; and the changes needed to improve student outcomes.
TASK	3	Management	The individual focuses on the processes and tasks of using the innovation and the best use of information and resources. Issues related to efficiency, organizing, managing, and scheduling dominate.
SELF	2	Personal	The individual is uncertain about the demands of the innovation, his or her adequacy to meet those demands, and/or his or her role with the innovation. The individual is analyzing his or her relationship to the reward structure of the organization, determining his or her part in decision making, and considering potential conflicts with existing structures or personal commitment. Concerns also might involve the financial or status implications of the program for the individual and his or her colleagues.
	1	Informational	The individual indicates a general awaremess of the innovation and interest in learning more details about it. The individual does not seem to be worried about himself or herself in relation to the innovation. Any interest is in impersonal, substantive aspects of the innovation, such as its general characteristics, effects, and requirements for use.
	0	Unconcerned	The individual indicates little concern about or involvement with the innovation.

Figure 11.2.

In behavioral terms, this might be considered a reinforcement hierarchy (Merrett & Musgrove, 2010), as it identifies what's actually important to the teacher at a given time. A new teacher's focus might move from basic issues and themselves to more complex issues and student outcomes as they become more seasoned. George, Hall, and Stiegelbauer (2006) provide this scale as an expression of these stages of concern:

Stages of Concern		Expressions of Concern
"Impact"	6	I have some ideas about something that would work even better.
	5	I would like to coordinate my effort with others, to maximize the innovation's effect.
	4	How is my use affecting my students?
"Task"	3	I seem to be spending all my time getting materials ready.
"Self"	2	How will using it affect me?
	1	I would like to know more about it.
"Unconcerned"	0	I am not concerned about it.

Figure 11.3.

Understanding what's relevant or reinforcing to the teacher is paramount. While you might want to dive right in and help a new teacher ask more complex questions in the classroom as a pinpoint, for example, he might initially be more concerned with how he'll be evaluated, where he should clock in, what he should bring to meetings, and how he should appropriately request time off when he's sick. Or, as in the example above, reducing misbehavior that's driving the teacher crazy would likely be an initial concern that immediately benefits "self" but is also clearly linked to future goals of student achievement.

Behavioral Cusps

As we discussed in chapter 7, behavioral cusps offer another opportunity to find valued pinpoints to target with your coachee. According to Rosales-Ruiz and Baer (1997), a behavioral cusp is "a behavior change that has consequences for the organism beyond the change itself, some of which may be considered important" (p. 537). For example, consider the young child who learns to crawl. Where they may have initially been confined to what reinforcement was within their immediate reach, they now can access a variety of reinforcement (e.g., getting to siblings, playing with the dog, retrieving their favorite toy from the toy box) that was previously unavailable. As a result, other behaviors might begin to take shape like social play, walking, or further developing fine motor skills.

The concept of a cusp encourages you to consider the future implications of a pinpointed behavior rather than focusing solely on the immediate impact. For example, asking effective questions is a behavioral cusp. It leads to a variety of other positive outcomes like:

- Increased student engagement
- Responses from students
- Critical thinking by students

- Improved student achievement
- Reduced misbehavior
- Ongoing assessment of student learning
- Adjustment of instruction
- Increased problem-solving ability

Increasing Precision through Task Analysis

In education, pedagogy taught to teachers is drawn from a large body of research that is presented and published across a variety of popular literature (e.g., Hattie, 2009; Marzano, 2007). This is of great benefit as it essentially provides a bank of instructional strategies that you can pull from.

For example, managing response rates is an instructional strategy recommended by Marzano. There is a great deal of literature available online as a resource to educators. Case in point, Learning Sciences International provides a description of managing response rates for educators in their Managing Response Rates table.

26. Managing Response Rates
The teacher uses response rate techniques to maintain student engagement in questions.
Teacher Evidence - Teacher uses wait time - Teacher uses response cards - Teacher has students use hand signals to respond to questions - Teacher uses choral response - Teacher uses technology to keep track of students' responses - Teacher uses response chaining
Student Evidence - Multiple students or the entire class responds to questions posed by the teacher - When asked, students can describe their thinking about specific questions posed by the teacher

Figure 11.4.

While this protocol contains a nice list of the elements teachers require to maintain engagement, it isn't an effective learning or coaching tool in and of itself. To make it effective, a precise description of each element should be broken down into its components (as LSI has done in other resources) and sequenced as a series of small behavioral steps. As you have learned, a task analysis is a powerful tool for training, coaching, and self-management. There are a few ways to develop it. One is to directly observe a master educator and then document their steps. Another is to study experts or consult them about performing the required task. And finally, if you are an expert in a particular skill, you can document your own steps as they're completed.

To illustrate, let's look at this example of a simple task analysis that might be used as a strategy for managing response rates.

Managing Response Rates	
Element	**Description**
Question	Begin by asking an open-ended question.
Wait time	Pause for approximately 10 seconds.
Calling on student	Randomly select a student.
Response	Ask student for the answer.

Figure 11.5.

Now you can easily continue this task analysis. For example:

- What should the teacher do if the student's answer is correct?
- What should the teacher do if the student's answer is partially correct?
- What should the teacher do if the student's answer is incorrect?

This information can be precisely described as part of the task analysis, used to train and coach management of response rates, used by teachers to remind them of what to do prior to instruction, or used by teachers as a self-assessment to determine how well they did after instruction. All of these marvelous performance-improvement tools blossom out of a good task analysis!

As the old saying goes, the devil is in the details. This is never more evident than when it comes to teaching. Sometimes teachers do the right thing at the wrong time. Sometimes they do the wrong thing at the right time. In both cases, precision is the issue. If the teacher calls on a student prior to asking the question in the task illustration above, the simple error in sequencing can have the unintended effect of disengaging the rest of the class. In other words, while the student who is called on must think about how to answer the question, other students might turn off their thinking caps as they now don't anticipate being called on. Asking the question first and then calling on a student, as indicated in the task analysis, is an effective strategy for engaging all of the students rather than just one. Once again, precision is king (or queen). When performing certain tasks, even one absent or incorrectly sequenced critical behavior (like making a right instead of a left) can have a ripple effect.

A final note regarding the number of steps or level of detail required of a task analysis. The key element to consider when developing it has to do with the skill level of the teacher as well as the teacher's prior experiences of learning or applying the skill. The greater the knowledge and skill, the less detail required.

Checklists

Most people are familiar with checklists. They're used for a variety of tasks like chores or shopping lists. While an unsophisticated means of remembering things, it is in fact a powerful tool for getting a variety of personal and professional tasks right. Used by a variety of professionals, including diligent surgeons, the development of the checklist is rooted in an unfortunate historical event (Gawande, 2010).

In 1935, after five years of development, the most sophisticated plane in aviation history sped down the runway, lifted off the pavement to begin ascent, then stalled and crashed in a fiery explosion that killed three people. Suspecting there was something wrong with the aircraft, investigators completed a thorough search. But to everybody's surprise, they found mechanical failure wasn't responsible for the crash. Human error was. As the plane became more sophisticated in its development, so did the techniques for flying it. Unfortunately, humans aren't infallible. Mistakes are a part of life. In most cases they can lead to learning, but in some cases, as in those related to flying or surgery, they can cost lives.

As a result of this unfortunate incident, the world witnessed the birth of the checklist, which is simply a task analysis that can be "checked" as steps happen. Checklists are powerful tools. They can be used for training, coaching, or even self-management. In a training intervention, teachers can review the checklist as they practice the sequence of steps. In coaching, coaches can use it to collect data and provide feedback to the teacher regarding the specific skills they got right and the ones they should deliberately focus on. And in self-management, deliberate coaches can assign the tool to teachers, who use it to remind themselves to implement a skill and assess their own performance afterward. In all cases, the checklist provides a metric that can help you continue to shape performance. To use it as a measure, one needs only to divide the number of steps executed correctly by the total number of steps. For example, if a teacher gets seven out of ten steps right, they have a score of 70 percent.

In the initial task analysis example above, we deliberately included a box that can be checked as an indicator that the teacher performed the step correctly, or in the correct sequence (see the Managing Response Rates table). In this example, the teacher gets three out of four steps correct—75 percent.

Precision in your coaching will keep you and your coachee focused on behaviors and results that matter. If you're too vague, any coaching interactions could simply be white noise to the teacher you're working with. If you can't specify the behavior you're trying to affect and why it's important, you can't expect the teacher to change or to know what they're doing well.

CHAPTER 12

PURPOSEFUL COACHING

A person who won't read has no advantage over one who can't read.
—Unknown

Long-lasting and efficient behavior change requires a planned, strategic approach. It must be purposeful, or intentionally designed with a focus on developing a few skills at a time through lots of repetition and feedback. This is especially important in an educational setting where students often have summers off with limited learning opportunities. If the skills taught to our students are not embedded into day-to-day activities (e.g., home skills, games, sports) or taught to fast and accurate fluency standards during the school year, then many of the skills won't last through summer. This means that an already short academic year gets shorter, using those first few weeks to get students caught up and back in the swing of learning. Add in breaks, testing, and sick days, and you can see why the time educators have is so precious.

To take advantage of that time, you have to be precise with your interactions—you don't have time for multiple thirty-minute coaching conversations with each teacher each day. So how do you choose a course of action? How do you know whether you should be modeling the correct behavior for the teacher, providing feedback, prompting a teacher to check the curriculum before a lesson, or any number of other potential coaching solutions? Going with the wrong solution isn't the end of the world, but it will waste the time we've already determined to be so valuable.

You choose by assessing why the behavior, good or bad, is occurring. Everyone knows Mrs. Barker is great at making the students laugh, but how exactly does Mrs. Barker do this? Why are there so many disruptions in Mr. Polerecky's class? Sadly, workplace performance has historically lacked an assessment of why behavior occurs (Austin, Carr, & Agnew, 1999). Without this knowledge, you're coaching blind, relying on a time-wasting trial-and-error approach. The science of behavior has made some advancements in this area over the years, most notably with the development and extended application of the Performance Diagnostic Checklist (Austin, 2000; Austin, Weatherly, & Gravina, 2005; Wilder, Lipschultz, King, Driscoll, & Sigurdsson, 2018). The Performance Diagnostic Checklist (PDC) is a short questionnaire that assesses what elements in the workplace are causing performance problems to occur. Well-researched versions of this assessment tool have been applied to human-services settings (Carr, Wilder, Majdalany, Mathisen, & Strain, 2013) and safety (Martinez-Onstott, Wilder, & Sigurdsson, 2016). The foundation of the various checklist versions spans four areas, based on the antecedent-behavior-consequence model that encompasses behavior change: antecedents and information, equipment and processes, knowledge and skills, and consequences.

1. *Antecedents and information.* Can the teacher explain to you exactly what they're supposed to be doing? Are there aids and prompts available to help the teacher know when and how to do it? These are types of antecedents that help get the behavior going. Educators need to have clear goals and expectations if you want them to meet your standards.
2. *Equipment and processes.* Does the teacher have reliable materials in the classroom? Are the classroom and school processes organized and efficient or complex and confusing? Are there any obstacles in the classroom that keep the teacher from doing their job well? School leaders need to set teachers up for success. You can't criticize a teacher for underperforming readers if there are no books to read!
3. *Knowledge and skills.* Can the teacher demonstrate the skill you're requiring of them? Can they do it reliably in the classroom environment when it's required? There is a big difference between attending a professional development event and actually demonstrating a skill. The number and quality of interactions during training, in particular opportunities to participate and to receive feedback and reinforcement, are critical to learning (Bucklin, Dickinson, & Brethower, 2000; Johnson & Rubin, 2011). Think about some of the training you've received. How much do you and your peers have to participate? Were you required to demonstrate mastery or fluency? If not, that training event most likely did little more than make you generally aware of the topics under discussion and didn't actually expand your day-to-day repertoire with new skills. If the teacher can't demonstrate the skill when asked, then you don't have anything to coach. You need to shift your focus to training those skills, then coaching the teacher to use those skills in the classroom.

4. *Consequences.* Once someone can demonstrate the skill and the environment isn't restricting them from consistently performing it at a high level, you're ready to make good things happen when that behavior occurs. Does the teacher get monitored? How often does the teacher receive positive feedback? What about constructive feedback? How often is constructive feedback followed up with positive reinforcement? Antecedents like training, task clarification, and prompts help set teachers up for success, but consequences show them that what you're asking of them actually matters.

The first three areas address whether someone actually *can do* the skill, whereas the "consequences" area addresses whether someone is capable of doing the skill but *won't*. For "can't do" (i.e., skill deficit), the intervention of choice should be linked to antecedent strategies like training. Unfortunately, too often teachers are told what to do but not actually taught through concise instruction, opportunities to demonstrate the skill, and consistent feedback.

To determine if a teacher has a skill deficit, ask them to describe the skill, then ask them to demonstrate it. If they can demonstrate it but it is slow, then the issue has to do with fluency and simply requires more opportunity to rehearse.

A teacher can be well trained on how to address problem behavior, know all the policies and procedures to support these actions, and demonstrate the proper thing to do, but still do something else when a student acts out during class. Why? Because what the teacher is doing works. That is, there are powerful consequences keeping these behaviors going.

For instance, after meeting with a multidisciplinary team to review behavior data of a student, it was determined that the child's off-task behavior was being maintained primarily by escape from work. Specifically, the child was avoiding math he was clearly capable of doing based on previous assessments. For almost the entire day, he was very well-behaved. However, during the math block, the student would reliably begin to drift off task and engage in a variety of other behaviors including drawing pictures, asking to go the bathroom, sharpening his pencil, or sometimes attempting to quietly chat with a peer.

When these behaviors initially happened, the teacher would quietly prompt the student back to task; however, after a while, the teacher became annoyed with the reccurring behaviors and began reprimanding. Initially this worked as the student returned to task; however, this strained the relationship between the student and the teacher as evidenced by a new behavior. Noncompliance. In other words, the student eventually stopped returning back to task based on the teacher's reprimand,

and even shouted at the teacher "why are you always picking on me!" This incident led the teacher to call the student's parents and request a meeting with the team.

After careful consideration, the team put a plan in place that required the teacher to break math assignments down into smaller chunks (e.g., providing half a page of math problems instead of a full page) and allowed the student a brief break. In addition, the student was given permission to quietly draw pictures *contingent* upon completing a prespecified amount of work that would be progressively increased over time. The team thanked the teacher for calling the meeting and the coach reminded her, "Don't forget, these plans can take some time to work. Give it a chance."

So the teacher set off with good intentions. She met with the student to discuss the plan as it pertained to her role and his. Per the plan, she would provide him encouragement just prior to the math block as a reminder of the contingency (e.g., "Don't forget, first do this work, then you can draw for 3 minutes. I know you can do it!"). She would then provide him with chunked work that he would then complete and return to her.

For the first week, the plan worked beautifully. However, problem behaviors began to rear their head again which prompted the teacher to reprimand. Like before, her reprimands initially worked, but then quickly lost their effect as the student returned to being noncompliant. After a quick observation using the plan as a checklist, the coach realized the teacher had omitted one pinpointed behavior in the plan; that is, she stopped providing the student chunked work because it required increased effort. So this led her to return to her primary behavior management tool that reliably worked for other students with infrequent misbehavior. It wasn't because the teacher was a bad teacher. It's because this behavior management tool reliably worked in the past. In other words, good things happened as a result. Students stopped misbehaving and the teacher escaped situations that interrupted her instruction.

And ironically, chunking the work was actually far less effort than managing the misbehavior, far less disrupting to the classroom, and far less frustrating to the teacher! When the teacher breaks protocol, it's the job of the coach to help teachers recognize that better things happen when he or she follows protocol. In other words, the intervention of choice for a motivation deficit should help them get in touch with positive outcomes as a result of correct performance. For example:

1. Providing the teacher with more frequent and reinforcing feedback (e.g., "I noticed you are following the plan by doing X, you are doing great!")
2. Helping the teacher see the positive impact of their behavior (e.g., "As a result of doing X, have you noticed the student is completing more work and disrupting less?")

3. Providing corrective feedback that is received by the teacher as helpful ("I noticed you chunked the student's work the first week, but you aren't doing it now. I understand this might seem like more effort, but remember, it's costing you far less frustration and time as compared with managing the misbehavior. You can do it! Would you like help chunking some of the material this week?")

In the scenario above, if the student had been acting out because he had a skill deficit related to math, the entire meeting and intervention would have been a waste of time. Moreover, the student would have likely continued acting out, perhaps with increased frequency and intensity; the teacher would have likely gotten more frustrated and disillusioned; and the coaching relationship may have been negatively impacted as the solution supported by the coach did not work. Below is a version of the Performance Diagnostic Checklist adapted for education (Gavoni & Rodriguez, 2016). If the folks you're coaching aren't performing well or achieving desired outcomes, this checklist will helps you to intervene effectively by first allowing you to determine the root cause of a performance issue prior to determining appropriate coaching interventions.

Performance Diagnostic Checklist—Education

(Gavoni & Rodriguez, 2016)

Teacher's Name: ________________ Interviewer: ____________________ Date: __________

Briefly describe performance concern:____

____

____

____

Training	YES	NO
Is there a written description telling exactly what is expected of the teacher regarding a particular instructional/behavioral strategy?		
Has the teacher received adequate instruction about what to do? ("I want you to do this and this before we leave today.")		
Has the teacher received formal training on this instructional/behavioral strategy? If yes, check all applicable training methods. Instructions ☒ Demonstration ☒ Rehearsal ☒		
Are there task aids visible *while* completing the instructional/behavioral strategy in question? (Task aids are reminders to prompt the strategy in the correct way at the correct time and for the correct duration.)		
Can the teacher state the purpose of the instructional/behavioral strategy?		

Figure 12.1.

continues ☒

Training	YES	NO
Is the teacher ever verbally, textually, or electronically reminded to use the instructional/behavioral strategy? If so, how often? Hourly ☒ Daily ☒ Weekly ☒ Monthly ☒ By whom? Check all that apply: Peer ☒ Coach ☒ Administrator ☒ Other ☒		
Are there frequently updated, challenging, and attainable goals that the teacher is comfortable with in relation to the instructional/behavioral strategy?		
Is the teacher aware of the mission of the school?		

Equipment and Processes	YES	NO
If equipment is required, is it available (e.g., computer, A/V, mic)? Is it in good working order?		
Are the equipment and environment optimally arranged (e.g., the arrangement of the students' desks)?		
Are larger processes performing well despite any incorrect instructional/behavioral strategies along the way (e.g., routines and procedures)?		
Are these processes arranged in a logical manner?		
Are teachers able to implement the instructional/behavioral strategy without any obstacles (e.g., interruption by the intercom)?		

Knowledge and Skills	YES	NO
Can the teacher tell you what he/she is supposed to be doing and how to do it?		
Can the teacher physically/verbally precisely demonstrate the instructional/behavioral strategy?		
If the instructional/behavioral strategy needs to be completed quickly, can the teacher perform it at the appropriate speed?		

Motivation	YES	NO
Are educators motivated based on the outcomes following completion of the task?		
Do teachers see the positive effects of implementing the instructional/behavioral strategy (e.g., increased student engagement, increased assessment data, decreased misbehavior)?		
How often do administrators monitor the teacher? Hourly ☒ Daily ☒ Weekly ☒ Monthly ☒		

Motivation	YES	NO
Does the teacher receive feedback about the performance? If so, By whom? ________________ How often? ________________ How long of a delay is there between the instructional/behavioral strategy and the delivery of feedback? ________________ Check all that apply. Feedback focus: Positive ☒ Constructive ☒ Feedback type: Written ☒ Verbal ☒ Graphed ☒ Other ☒		
Is the instructional/behavioral strategy particularly effortful or difficult?		
Do other instructional/behavioral strategies (elements) appear to take precedence over the targeted strategy? If yes, indicate the strategies below. Element #: ________________ Element #: ________________ Element #: ________________ Element #: ________________		

A Note on Performance Evaluations

In education, performance evaluations tend to occur semiannually. As a result they have little impact on performance improvement and really serve as a documented summary of what the teacher should already know. Because of the time involved and negative impact on staff morale, many believe the process actually impedes rather than helps performance. Some even consider the aggregate of performance evaluations as the ultimate measurement of coaching (leadership). In other words, the more effective the coaching, the more likely the teachers and staff will succeed.

Aubrey Daniels, the godfather of organizational behavior management, suggests that the most satisfied teachers are those who know at the end of the day how well they performed so there are never any surprises. In other words, when it comes time for their formal evaluation, teachers and staff should already have a good idea of how they're performing.

To help teachers reach their maximum potential, coaches should always remember these five essentials:

1. *Align outcomes with pinpointed behaviors.* Teachers should know exactly what result they are working toward, and exactly what they should be doing to achieve that result.
2. *Track performance.* Teachers should be provided measurement that allows them to gauge how well they're performing. For example, on

the academic side there are a variety of measures, including formative assessments, standardized assessments, and daily behavior data. At the school level, leading indicators like student attendance, staff attendance, benchmark data, and discipline data can serve as measures of schoolwide progress.

3. *Don't forget the "why."* Figure out why teachers are doing what they're doing, both good and bad. They're doing it for a reason, and knowing what that reason is will help guide your coaching.
4. *Feedback.* Measurement isn't any good if the teachers don't know about it. In professional sports, a variety of data is collected on individual and team performance. Imagine a professional football team having no information about the score, where they are on the field, what down it is, or how much time is left in the quarter. They won't know which way is up! Measurement toward goals should be shared with teachers weekly, no later than monthly. Feedback on their behavior should be provided as often as possible. The most successful supervisors and managers provide feedback as immediately as they can. Feedback should be behaviorally specific and provided at a 4:1 ratio. That is, four positive statements recognizing appropriate behavior or incremental improvements to one constructive statement providing information that helps the performer improve. Supervisors who attempt to correct behavior more than they attempt to recognize and reinforce it will find themselves surrounded by unhappy teachers.
5. *Reinforcement.* Celebrate success as teachers reach established subgoals and goals weekly and/or monthly; reinforce behaviors daily that lead toward those goals.

You might be thinking, "How can I get measurement and feedback to the group of teachers I manage or supervise?" Well, each of you will have your own approach. Some coaches have strong habits linked to the use of measurement and feedback. Still others are working on their habits. One simple strategy that's gaining momentum is called the Big Five Performance Management system (Ferguson, 2013). Here's how it works. Each month, teachers submit a monthly email message to their coach describing two things:

1. Their five most significant accomplishments from last month in a one- or two-sentence statement
2. Their five highest priorities for the current month

This process takes no more than ten minutes per month, but it gives teachers a chance to tell their story and take credit for their contributions. As a result, managers have the opportunity to affirm, guide, and even redirect their efforts toward goals that you've both agreed on and that are aligned in the appraisal system. While providing regular documentation of your attempts to support performance improvement, it also improves the quality and quantity of your coaching efforts. This strategy can be linked to your school's teacher appraisal and alignment tool, keeping your team members strategically focused on their highest priorities. You can require your reports to submit emails each month on the fifth calendar day to help with consistency and double down on the idea of the "Big Five." Here's what it might look like:

To: Jane Smith From: Sharonda Murphy

March Accomplishments

- Helped JM learn how to request a break.
- Worked with the team to redevelop LM's goals.
- Researched an engagement strategy (choral responding) and began using it.
- Personally met with 3 families to update them on their child's progress.
- Helped Mary, my colleague, learn how to develop a lesson plan.

April Priorities

- Focus on asking rather than telling my students to foster more critical thinking.
- Seek out more feedback from leadership and colleagues on my own performance.
- Research another strategy related to engagement.
- Schedule a meeting with 3 more families to update them on their child's progress.
- Prepare a de-escalation training for the upcoming parent training day.

Figure 12.2.

As you can see, the process is simple. In this example, when April rolls around, the teacher simply needs to cut and paste the April priorities into the next email and reflect on their accomplishments as related to these goals, then set priorities for May. All the coach needs to do is provide a quick affirmation of accomplishments where warranted, then give guidance or redirection where necessary.

For example, "Thanks for a great March! Keep up the good work, especially with those parent meetings. You've really improved with your frequency of these. Don't forget, progress reports are due next week. It's our goal to get 100 percent of them in by April 8." In other cases, after you've affirmed any accomplishments, you might simply state, "I'm not sure I agree with the focus of your parent training for next month. Please come see me so we can discuss before you begin."

You can also include thought-provoking questions several times a year in your responses. For example, "In your Big Five this month, please answer the following question: If you ran this school differently, what would be one thing you'd do to improve our customer service?"

Now that we've provided you with some tips, let's get started!

CHAPTER 13

SYSTEMATIC COACHING

A goal without a plan is just a wish.

—Antoine de Saint-Exupery

The Deliberate Coaching approach is a targeted and systematic approach. It is planned and strategic but also dynamic, designed to build, adapt, and produce demonstrable results in key areas of the learning process and classroom. Our schools are filled with educational and support systems working together to produce educated and respectable young people. Because these systems are dynamic, our methods must be dynamic. Because these systems are demanding, our teacher-management approaches must be organized and strategic so that we don't lose sight of where we're going (outcomes and linked teacher behaviors) and how we need to get there (coaching).

A Consistent Path to Excellence

Skinner (1953) once described how a scientific approach to behavior "shapes behavior as a sculptor shapes a lump of clay" (p. 91). The coach as sculptor shapes the behavior of a particular teacher by consistently working to support that teacher toward an ultimate performance goal. Good teachers are not born. Educators do not begin their careers with an innate ability to get the most out of their students. These behaviors need to be built, molded over time. Take something as seemingly simple as the affect someone displays when speaking to a child. The pitch, proximity to the child, words used, and so on all need to be developed, either naturally through contingencies in the environment (e.g., by the child's reaction) or by a coach. Someone's first attempt at interacting with a child might fail miserably. The child might not respond to the person, walk away, or do something disruptive. So you work with the person, reinforcing small improvements until they can finally speak to the child in an appropriate manner. Shaping behavior must be deliberate, and it must be planned and consistent or the previously reinforced behavior will go away (or more formally, it will be extinguished).

The same goes for tasks that involve numerous interlinked behaviors. These behavior chains must be reinforced systematically and supported until you get to the final performance goal. Before a teacher can appropriately troubleshoot a struggling student's problem and assist, they must first get comfortable interacting with students, showing them that they care and have something of value to contribute. We sometimes say this is a period of time when a teacher "pairs" themself with reinforcement, meaning that the student sees that good things happen when that teacher is around. Once this is done, the teacher needs to be able to identify struggling students, noticing signs and opportunities for improvement. Then the teacher must be able to determine why the student is struggling, select the proper solution, and assist the student until progress is made.

Because behavior occurs through reinforcement, and because behavior stops if reinforcement stops, coaches must be mindful of how and when they're offering support to teachers. Educators don't have a lot of time during the day to spare, so in order for coaching to be consistent, it has to be brief. And to maximize performance and avoid extinction of new and critical behaviors, coaching must also be frequent.

The 8 Ws: The Deliberate Plan

Measure twice, cut once. Systematic coaching has a direction. It's organized. You're taking the time to figure out what you're going to do, how you're going to do it, and why you're going to do it. This enables informed decision-making. It helps with your shaping process. All of these are valuable to optimize your time as a coach.

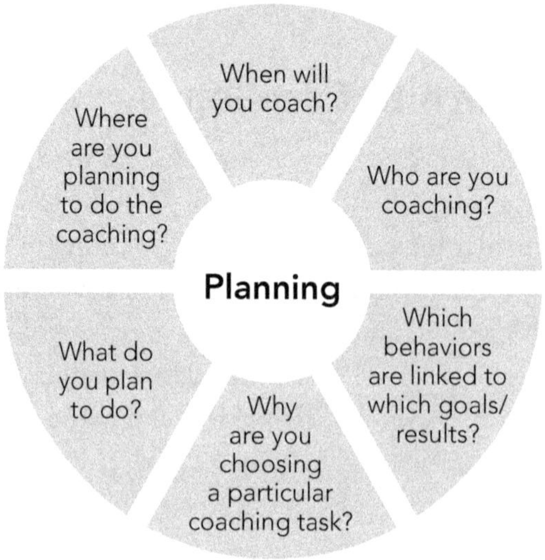

Figure 13.1.

The 8 Ws: The Deliberate Interaction

Plan the work and work the plan. Try to be quick in your interactions so as not to waste time. This will also allow you to increase the frequency of your coaching interactions. Everything you do as a coach funnels down to the coaching interaction. Your observations help you find your pinpoints: what is important to the classroom, what is important to the teacher, what are the behaviors that are working, and what are the behaviors that are not working? You need this information to know where performance is and where it needs to be. You need it to guide your feedback statements, ensuring precision. Your assessment tells you what you're supposed to do during your coaching interaction. Do you need to ask questions to find the reason for a performance deficit? Do you need to model to help build a skill? Do you need to provide constructive feedback to get a new behavior going? Do you need to provide any follow-up reinforcement? Everything in your assessment leads to your coaching interaction.

Figure 13.2.

The 8 Ws: The Deliberate Review

Systematic ongoing review will help a coach see the path to good teaching habits. When you have a behavior you need to shape, shaping takes monitoring and consistency. You want a teacher interacting with their students frequently, specifically, and positively, for instance, so you first build the starting behavior up, increasing the frequency of interactions. Once you consistently have more frequent interactions, you build up the quality of those interactions. As you get closer to the final behavior you're looking for, you start to only reinforce the behaviors that more closely resemble it.

Similarly, if you have a behavior that you want to go away, correcting it will only take you so far. You might get rid of one undesired behavior, then find another one in its place. And this is no fault of the teacher. If the teacher doesn't know what else to do, they'll try something that may or may not work. As the coach, you need to replace the incorrect behavior with another behavior. This requires follow-up, which continues until you build the replacement behavior, linking it to natural reinforcers.

Seeing Progress to Reinforce Progress

According to a popular saying, you don't know where you're going until you know where you've been. Coaches can't coach if they don't know what they're coaching and how it's impacting performance. That's how we show the value of what we do—we need to track performance to see it. Teachers show value the same way, with others judging it based on the performance of their students. But vice principals, principals, and other school coaches are only in a position to get a snapshot of what the teachers are doing to get that performance.

You don't know where you're going until you know where you've been.

A recent survey conducted by the ROI Institute sought the opinions of executives on training and development. Targeting CEOs of Fortune 500 organizations and large private firms, it provided a unique glimpse into the mindset of the individuals responsible for funding our training efforts. The survey covered various topics reported by their training and development departments, such as how highly employees rate the training, the impact training has on top business metrics, training efficiency, return on investment (ROI), and how much employees learn as a result of the training. According to the CEOs, the two factors their training departments considered most significant were the number of employees trained in a given year and the training efficiency (e.g., cost per hour of learning). Coincidentally, these were also at the *bottom* of the CEOs' list. Instead, they believed that the *impact* of training on key business metrics and ROI (cost/benefit) were among the most important factors. And what reports did the CEOs report receiving the least? You guessed it—impact metrics and ROI.

Why are these findings so important? They show that it's easy to ignore the message we're trying to send with our outcomes. As a coach, do you know what the school administration looks at to see the value in what you're doing? As a school administrator do you know what the school board looks at to see the value in what you do? What about parents and key stakeholders in the community? Our school systems are just that: *systems*. Particularly, they are *performance systems*, requiring resources and support to guide the individuals responsible for producing results. Noted in the CEO survey was that the chief learning officer—the head of training and development—is approximately three levels below the CEO, leaving a sizeable hill to climb to provide and maintain support. How far removed are you from the key decision-makers in your school district, those individuals responsible for giving you the resources and flexibility you need to be a successful coach? Sustainable support and growth in our school systems comes when we show that our work adds value that's greater than the cost required to attain meaningful results. Specifically, we must show value in a precise, objective, and replicable way.

The Coaching Telephone Game

Consider this scenario. You're walking down the hallway to pick your child up from daycare when you see a group of kids circling their teacher in anticipation. The teacher whispers something in the ear of the child closest to her and asks her to pass it along. The girl whispers in the ear of the boy next to her, who then does the same to the boy next to him, and so on until the final child gets the message. At this point the teacher asks the last child to recite the message: "No planks hidden in the monsoon," the child says with confidence. "And Olivia, what was the message I gave you?" Olivia laughs and says, "Snowflakes will fall softly soon."

What does the telephone game have to do with your coaching system? Let me paint you a picture of the *coaching* telephone game:

1. School decision-makers want to invest in people and systems that add value to the school.
2. To get an idea of what has value and what doesn't, they'll either be *told* or be *shown*.
3. If you don't report directly to these decision-makers as a coach, this means you have to find a way to relay the information up the chain of command. If you rely on subjective descriptions and verbal reports, you're leaving your impact up to interpretation. By the time it gets to the school decision-makers, they might be wondering how "planks and monsoons" are worth the school's continued support.

What to Do Instead

The Deliberate Coaching process is designed to allow small tweaks in the way you affect teacher performance. However, this process still requires support from senior school leaders. These key individuals are essential to ensuring that your impact is maximized for as long as you're with the school. Think of the behaviors you want from these individuals. Perhaps you want them to sign off on assigning or hiring more coaches, buy more materials, or follow through on suggestions you made about how to properly utilize your coaching recommendations. If these behaviors are to occur, then they, like all other behaviors, need motivation—something you can reinforce by following a few suggestions:

#1. Train for Impact

To demonstrate value up the chain of command, you must control your message. You do this by pinpointing critical metrics in a way that is objective. Precision is key here. This enables you to clearly present your value in the form of concise, objective impact data and reports. Think of the numbers that come up in discussions of how much your school is progressing or how strong a particular teacher is. These could be things like standardized test scores, the cost of student progress, expenses, or teacher retention. These impact data will not only help you control your value message, but they'll also help guide your coaching efforts and allow you to continuously improve your coaching systems, staying one step ahead by tracking the most critical metrics.

Identifying critical impact results is important, but getting results for things like performance evaluations, turnover data, and school costs can take time—valuable time that you could spend making appropriate adjustments and fine-tuning your coaching to ensure that those delayed results will show something positive. You need more leading indicators of success, things like teachers' day-to-day attendance and timeliness, curriculum adjustments, student progress, or teacher feedback surveys. You find these by starting with the lagging metrics that show what is important to the school (like graduation rates and teacher turnover), yet are taken too infrequently to use as a primary way to show what is working and what is not. From these lagging indicators you can then identify the leading indicators that you have a constant and direct impact on. This frequent tracking allows you to identify strengths of your coaching and areas that need improvement. By impacting these leading indicators, you'll be able to proactively ensure that you'll have a positive impact on the infrequent results that are most critical to the school and the school decision-makers.

#2. Tracking the Behavior Leads to Result Alignment

As you track progress, your goal is to showcase how the critical teacher behaviors you're coaching are impacting results that matter. As individuals responsible for teacher development, your job is to build these behaviors. If you build the wrong behaviors, you risk spending time and money on skills that fail to have an effect on anything, ultimately producing unhappy school administrators who might not support your next initiative.

Depending on your role, you might be responsible for your school's training and coaching systems or at least have access to the person who does. Regardless, start off by identifying the teacher behaviors that will have the greatest impact on the critical measures of success you're tracking for the school, classroom, and students. If you don't know what these behaviors are, then ask. Better to find a group of exemplars and find out what they do to be successful than guess or try to remember what you used to do prior to your promotion. These teachers are responsible for the work, whereas their supervisors are responsible for *influencing* the work. You can make the greatest impact on your key performance outcomes by prioritizing those doing the work. So if you can identify the right teacher behaviors to coach—those that have a clear link to critical results—you'll be ready to develop a plan to target those behaviors. Without truly knowing what those behaviors are, you're leaving your coaching (and potentially your job) up to chance . . . and that's not good science!

If you're responsible for training and coaching teachers, then you might also be responsible for training other coaches and leaders. For this group, continue aligning critical behaviors and results to identify the key leadership behaviors that have the greatest impact on the performance of the teachers. Again, if you don't know what those behaviors are, find the exemplars and ask them to describe how they've achieved success as a leader.

But a word of caution from your friendly neighborhood behavior analysts. It's imperative that you don't just find people who get the best results. A bad leader can get good results in the wrong way, and you don't want to create an army of these individuals. It's easy to fall into the trap of assuming that just because Bill has been a vice principal for twenty years and seems to get the results the school is looking for, his do-it-or-else approach to leadership is something to replicate. In the same regard, you also don't necessarily want to find the manager who is the most liked. You want to create a team of leaders who know how to lead, not just be your friend. The sweet spot is the leader who gets results in the right way. These are the supportive and proactive leaders who lead by positively reinforcing good performance. Find these individuals and ask them to describe what they do to be effective. Just as you did when identifying your results, you're looking for specific pinpointed behaviors that can be measured. Ask the leader questions like "What does *leading by example* look like?" to really find the behaviors. Vague descriptions of behavior that lack precision and focus will produce vague coaching systems that lack precision and focus.

#3. Demonstrate Value with Measurement

One of the most powerful tools in your science toolbox is your measurement system. Good data help take away the murky bias of subjectivity and allow for a breath of objective fresh air. Here are a few stories that might help showcase the value of tracking and aligning your impact.

Matt's Story

Matt is responsible for professional development at his school and has heard great things about his training and coaching. After the number of positive reports decrease, he decides that his systems need an overhaul. Now he's getting more complaints than ever. He's always been against relying on data to show that his leadership works, confident in his process and impact. But his confidence is starting to waver.

What Matt Should Do

Measurements and data are there to tell a story. When it comes to measuring the impact of your coaching system, they're here to tell *your* story. They should be embraced for their reinforcement and decision-making potential, not rejected.

Matt was relying on the coaching telephone game to evaluate his coaching, then using this information to guide serious changes in his leadership system. If you're not tracking progress, this approach can result in costly errors. You might continue to replicate an ineffective training only to later find out that your training is missing the mark. Even worse, you could stop or change an *effective* coaching system because of anecdotal or subjective reports that have nothing to do with your true training impact.

Sue's Story

Sue is a principal who's also failing to see meaningful change. Unlike Matt, she's been tracking impact metrics. Historically, her adherence to the annual budget targets, coupled with her school's pristine graduation rate, has shown the kind of results that make her school a highly regarded asset for the district. But recent layoffs, budget cuts, and unexpected policy changes have left her in high demand, and her impact metrics are taking a turn for the worse.

What Sue Should Do

Sue is losing control of her impact. There are always going to be lagging metrics caused by variables that you and your teachers have little to no influence over. You can't control district-level policy changes that negatively affect your day-to-day operations, and you can't prevent layoffs and budget cuts that can affect classroom ratios, materials, and your school's overall fiscal and academic strength. However, you *can* control how you choose to measure and evaluate your impact as a leader and the impact of those coaches working with you. Remember that leading indicators are designed to help you not only continuously refine your coaching, but also present an accurate message to the district on the impact and value of these efforts. Sue hasn't been tracking leading indicators of her coaching impact, instead relying solely on lagging metrics—specifically the lagging metrics she had little control over. Without leading metrics, her message is intertwined with lagging results that don't fully capture her impact. Avoid relying on impact metrics that are outside of the control of your teachers and staff.

John's Story

John seems to be a step ahead of the rest. As a vice principal, he discusses how he's reduced teacher tardiness and made timely curriculum improvements over the past few months, and he reports that his feedback from teachers has been consistently positive. His troubles come when his principal pulls him aside to discuss the impact of his coaching. It turns out that standardized test scores have been declining and the number of student suspensions is up. The district is requesting that his coaching system be revised to address these issues.

What John Should Do

Unlike Sue, John has tracked both leading and lagging metrics. But while he's used his leading metrics to help his teachers and evaluate his own impact, he hasn't shared those metrics with his principal. He's also failed to track other critical outcomes to ensure that they aren't being neglected. Allowing decision-makers to act based on incomplete information can be costly.

Let your data tell the story so you can see what's working and why, then expand the value of these effective systems. Help your school find the true cause of a problem so it doesn't stop the one system that actually works. When your leading indicators are well pinpointed and linked to the right behaviors, you can demonstrate that the cause of subpar lagging results might not be poor training or coaching. If you don't have a seat at that table when discussing your impact, try to ensure that your data do.

Showcasing the link between key results and the behaviors you're coaching is just as important as the effectiveness of the coaching itself. Long-term administrative support depends on our training and coaching efforts remaining on the radar of key decision-makers. By understanding the expected impact of your leadership system, you can work to find the critical behaviors that should be guiding your coaching efforts. If you don't know the behaviors that lead to valued impact, you can't reliably build them. Our goal is valued results that can be reliably replicated, effectively disseminated, and clearly communicated.

CHAPTER 14

TAKING THAT FIRST STEP

If we hope to give our children a change, it's time we start giving our teachers a chance.

—Barack Obama

As you're considering how to bring together all you've learned, there must be a first step. You may do this by initially setting goals. However, you may have an inner voice telling you "I'm too busy." Still, you might try a few things out. Perhaps you'll show a few of these tools to your colleagues. But soon you may fall back into your old habits. If you find yourself there, remember this. People don't reach goals, no matter how small, when they fail to consistently engage in the behaviors that will lead them there. If you value something, you must first learn to recognize the behaviors that will lead you toward your goals, as well as recognize the behaviors that will lead you away from them. Reaching goals and successfully applying Deliberate Coaching principles with an individual, grade group, or school requires you to begin by deliberately doing something more, less, or differently. When you do this, you can effectively help the teachers you are supporting do the same to achieve their own success. Remember, all results are achieved by behavior. It's not magic. It's simply deliberate and consistent behavior. Time is often not at the root cause of failing to reach goals. It's typically what people do with their time that leads people to come up short. So if you want to achieve goals and help those you are coaching be successful, get out of your mind (i.e., thinking "I'm too busy") and get into your behaviors, one step at a time.

One thing to consider when determining which behaviors to begin with is assessing your current strengths and areas for improvement. There are things that you do as a coach that teachers like, teachers respond to, and work. You need to continue these things. There are also small improvements you can start making. You might need to adjust how often you see the teacher, engaging in more quick, frequent interactions and fewer long, infrequent feedback sessions. You also might consider how specific you are when you speak about teacher performance to clarify the behaviors you wish to change. We've offered a self-assessment tool that you can use to help identify some strengths and opportunities in your individual coaching. The assessment is broken down into areas of coaching, providing feedback, advising, and development planning. Your score can help guide you on the good practices you need to integrate into your long-term coaching.

Coaching Self-Assessment and Checklist

Perhaps you are new to the concept of coaching, or maybe you are a seasoned pro. Either way, use this sheet to periodically check yourself against core competencies that are essential to building a culture of coaching.

Point scale: 0 = never, 1 = only when requested by employees, 2 = inconsistently, 3 = at regular intervals (once or twice a year), 4 = as often as possible.

Please rate your skills on the following questions. Then, star two areas where you feel you have strength as a coach, and check two area where you would like to improve your coaching.

Coaching (listen and draw out)

Talk with employees about what they like most about work (not necessarily just their current job)	
Listen to employees, concerns about the progress and direction of their careers	
Learn what is motivating for your employees	
Step out of the "expert" role and truly listen, just to understand your employee's perspective	

Reality testing (provide positive and corrective feedback)

Recognize and reward employees for their contributions, in the presence of others	
Initiate discussions with your employees about how you see their future career	
Explain formal and informal factors that determine success in the organization	

Advising (offer organizational insight, information, and advice)

Talk clearly about changes in the organization that will require new learning	
Offer suggestions for opportunities for new learning	
Work to identify on-the-job opportunities for your employees (inside and outside your immediate area) that are in line with organizational goals and employee desires	
Provide resources for employees who want information on developmental opportunities	

Development planning (guide employee goal setting, check back)	
Review and discuss an employee's written professional development plan and goals	
Discuss expectations (yours and theirs) regarding professional development planning	
Check in with employees about their progress on development goals/initiatives	
Provide physical support (money, time off, personal assistance) for employees to pursue more learning	
Provide motivational support for employees to pursue more learning	

Figure 14.1.

Social Validity in Deliberate Coaching

One of the guiding principles behind Deliberate Coaching is *social validity.* In the world of behavior analysis, social validity is defined by the following three components (Wolf, 1978):

1. Social significance of the goals of treatment
2. Social appropriateness of the treatment procedure
3. Social importance of the effects of treatment

You might be thinking, "What the heck does *treatment* have to do with coaching? Treatment to most folks usually means a doctor treating a patient to help them get better." Well, let's take a deeper albeit quick look at the term. Dictionary.com defines treatment as:

1. An act or manner of treating
2. An action or behavior toward a person, animal, etc.
3. Management in the application of medicine, surgery, etc.

If we take a few liberties and substitute "coaching" in the definition, it looks like this when applied to education:

1. An act or manner of coaching a teacher
2. A coaching action or behavior toward a teacher
3. Management in the application of coaching

It's easy to see how Deliberate Coaching might be considered a type of "treatment," as it's an approach and application of strategies intended to help teachers perform better. If we return to the concept of social validity, Carter (2010) defines it as "The evaluation of the degree of acceptance for the immediate variables associated with a procedure or program designed to change behavior" (p. 2). Simply put in terms of Deliberate Coaching, it's a measure of a person's reaction to or perception of the coaching. In order to continue applying Deliberate Coaching, it must not only be effective (e.g., having a positive impact on student achievement), but it must be considered relevant to the teachers, be provided in a way that engages them, and produce outcomes that are valued by the stakeholders. So if we return to the above three components as defined by Wolf (1978) but substitute the term "treatment" with "coaching," it meets the criteria we spoke of and looks like this:

1. Social significance of the goals (pinpoints) of coaching
2. Social appropriateness of the coaching procedure
3. Social importance of the effects of coaching

If your Deliberate Coaching approach isn't socially valid, you won't bring out the best in the teachers you serve. In fact, you might be lucky to simply get compliance, and you'll only get that when you're there providing direction. As soon as you leave the room, they'll likely go back to what they were doing before you stepped foot in their classroom. Because of this, it's important that you measure the reaction or perception of those you're coaching so you can continue to monitor and improve your Deliberate Coaching.

How can you determine the social validity of your coaching? Easily—ask those you coach! Here are some tools to help you along the way, based on *The Social Validity Manual: A Guide to Subjective Evaluation of Behavior Interventions* (Carter, 2010). You can provide these to individual teachers and use the aggregate data to determine trends related to how people perceive your coaching.

Rate your agreement/disagreement with each of the statements below for the following coaching pinpoints

Coaching Pinpoints	**1**	**2**	**3**	**4**	**5**	**6**
This is the best coaching pinpoint that could be chosen.						
This coaching pinpoint focuses on the most important issues.						
This coaching pinpoint increases the opportunity to improve in other areas.						
This is a reasonable coaching pinpoint to accomplish.						
This coaching pinpoint will not have a negative impact.						
This coaching pinpoint will increase opportunities for reinforcement.						
This coaching pinpoint is needed more than most other pinpoints.						

1 = Strongly Disagree; 2 = Disagree; 3 = Slightly Disagree; 4 = Slightly Agree; 5 = Agree; 6 = Strongly Agree

Figure 14.2. Determining social significance of the coaching pinpoints

Rate your agreement/disagreement with each of the statements below for the following coaching goals.						
Coaching Goals	**1**	**2**	**3**	**4**	**5**	**6**
I feel confident in my understanding of the coaching procedures.						
The coaching procedures are acceptable and ultimately linked to student outcomes.						
I am willing to follow through on the coach's recommendations.						
Given your needs and the needs of the students in my classroom, I find the coaching to be reasonable.						
The coaching I am receiving has been effective toward improving pinpointed skills.						
The coaching I am receiving is having a positive impact on pinpointed results.						
Following the coach's recommendation requires little effort from me.						
1 = Strongly Disagree; 2 = Disagree; 3 = Slightly Disagree; 4 = Slightly Agree; 5 = Agree; 6 = Strongly Agree						

Figure 14.3. Social appropriateness and importance of the coaching

As we've mentioned before, Deliberate Coaching requires purpose or intention. That said, always remember this: People won't judge you by your intentions, but rather your impact. While you may possess strong knowledge and good intentions, your coaching needs to be received well by those you're coaching. Social validity measures help you determine if it is, guiding your approach.

Coaching the Coaches

It's important to note that the Deliberate Coaching process can and should be applied at all levels of the school. If you are senior leader in your district or school, you will have likely identified school outcomes that are important, aligned those school outcomes with classroom outcomes, and aligned those classroom outcomes with the behaviors that teachers need to engage in to achieve them. Hopefully you've gone on to implement a Deliberate Coaching system where the leaders in the school who are responsible for teacher performance use tools like the 8 Ws to frequently and consistently support each teacher's progress toward hitting their classroom goals.

But don't forget about supporting the leaders who support the teachers! Any new leadership tool, process, or overall system is going to take some getting used to. Even though we recommend starting small, simply trying to tweak how leaders interact with teachers and then moving to frequency, consistency, quality, and the use of tools, this is still a new process. And new processes mean you're taking leaders out of their comfort zone, away from things that have occurred for a while because they've seen some sort of value in those things, and asking more of them. This adds a level of effort and uncertainty, both of which are going to compete with the new coaching behaviors you're looking for (those outlined in this book) and make the current behaviors you're trying to improve seem more appealing. In other words, change can be tough, so it's easy to stay with what you're currently doing.

Those responsible for the performance of the coaches need to recognize this. Those doing the reinforcing need reinforcement too!

Who?

Who are you coaching? Perhaps you're a principal coaching a vice principal or a vice principal coaching a district coach.

Which?

Which behaviors are linked to which goals and results? This book has identified a number of behaviors that are associated with successful coaches. A coach is indirectly responsible for the results of a classroom and directly responsible for the behaviors of the teacher. Which of these behaviors are your targets during your coaching for this particular week? What teacher outcomes is this behavior linked to? Perhaps you're focused on the quality of the feedback statement provided from a vice principal to a teacher, or whether the vice principal follows up with the teacher as planned after previous constructive feedback. Their providing feedback might be important because the teacher's performance is linked to a particular student-achievement area. Keeping this alignment when you're coaching the coaching helps you and the coach understand what you're supporting and why this is important.

Why?

Why are you choosing a particular coaching task? You might be observing the vice principal providing feedback so you can see exactly what components she's giving during the feedback conversation and how the teacher is reacting to the feedback. Or your target coaching behaviors for that week could be assessing what's working and what's not working with the vice principal to find out why the coach might be struggling in a certain area. Just as when you're coaching the teacher, this is important because you want to maximize the use of your time. You do this by ensuring that this is truly a skill-deficit problem and not a problem that should be addressed with prompting or consequences. Most likely there will only be a few people available to coach at your school and a lot of teachers who need coaching, so maximizing (and limiting) how much time you spend with them will be appreciated!

When?

When will you coach? Based on the aforementioned issue of time constraints, it's important to figure out the best time for your coaching. The sooner you can meet with the coach after the coach has an opportunity to engage in the behavior you're targeting the better. Remember that delayed consequences are less effective, and by delaying you also make it more likely that the coach will forget important details about the interaction. If you're not directly observing the coach in action, then what you're left with is reinforcing their account of that interaction. You need reliable information.

Where?

Where are you coaching? If you can't observe and engage with the coach in the environment they're coaching in without sacrificing the integrity of their coaching and privacy, then arrange to have a private place where you can meet shortly after. You don't want to accidentally find yourself providing feedback and having a coaching discussion in public. This will backfire quickly, even if you're simply providing praise.

What?

This is the point in the 8 Ws where you're planning for what you'll be doing and also recording what you *actually* did. Remember that this form is supposed to be used as an antecedent to guide your coaching, helping you hit the steps that are critical for success. For example, it might say that you're supposed to find the vice principal on Wednesday after her observation session with Mr. Clark and ask questions about how this session went in order to find opportunities for positive or constructive feedback. Once the coaching interaction is completed, you'll track what you actually ended up saying. This gives you a starting point for assessing how your coaching went and acts as a record in case *your* supervisor would like to discuss *your* coaching!

What Happened?

What was the impact? How do you know that the coaching has been successful? Part of tracking your process is ensuring that you know whether your coaching is working. This can be a potential reinforcer for you, it's a way for you to show your supervisor the success you're having, and it gives you something extra to focus on if you need to discuss various areas of success with your vice principal or whatever coach you're supervising. Your impact includes various results and outcomes, including the behavior of the coach you're coaching, the behavior of the teacher they're coaching, and any classroom changes you might be seeing. It also should include any notes you have on how the coach is taking your coaching. Do they seem to be asking you more questions? This is good. Do they seem to be approaching you more to share examples of their coaching? This is *very* good! How is their body language? Are they deflecting your feedback? The direction of their behavior change will tell you whether you're having a reinforcing or punishing effect. These additional notes will help paint a picture of how much they're valuing your coaching conversations.

Why Don't …?

"Why don't you follow up by prompting the teacher and let me know how that goes?" Think about what you'll do next. Just as when coaching teachers, coaching coaches doesn't stop. You continue until the coach's specific targets are met and you feel they're occurring at a high-enough level, and linked to enough natural consequences (the coach is doing it without you because it works), to move on to new targets. If you're shaping behavior, then your next steps will be finding the next level of that behavior in relation to the goal behavior. For example, the coach is meeting with teachers more often, but the meetings are still too long and vague. The next step in this case is to focus on the quality of the coaching interactions between the coach and the teacher. Tell the coach, "If your coaching interaction for that particular instance is constructive, then why don't you follow up later that week with some positive reinforcement for the replacement behavior?" Continuity is the key to sustainable growth.

Next Steps

Figure 14.4.

Even after all these decades of research, the beauty of the science behind behavior is that we're still impacting behaviors using our understanding of basic principles, our ABCs (antecedents-behaviors-consequences). Behavioral analysis can answer questions about why students are performing at their level, why teachers are teaching at their level, and even why the school district and legislators are making certain decisions. Although not always easy, there is a way to discover why people do what they do. The Deliberate Coaching process is one built on science and respect. Science to ensure the principles guiding teacher and coach performance are sound, and respect for those who have dedicated their lives to helping the children in our schools succeed. Training teachers is important to ensure they have the skills needed to effectively engage students in the learning process. Administrative support in school is critical to ensure there are processes, procedures, equipment, and standards in place to allow teachers and students to thrive. But coaching is needed to ensure long-term success. We hope the tools and processes in this book will provide a foundation to maximize teacher performance in a way that positively impacts your school culture and student achievement. Teachers deserve recognition (positive reinforcement) for the good work they do and frequent support to help them achieve their goals as educators. Coaches deserve recognition and support for shaping the teacher performance along the way. This process can't be random, it must be precise, systematic, and purposeful. It must be deliberate!

REFERENCES

Alessi, G. (1987). Generative strategies and teaching for generalization. *The Analysis of Verbal Behavior, 5*, 15–27.

Almeida, A. P. (2010). Classroom questioning: Teachers' perceptions and practices. *Procedia Social and Behavioral Sciences, 2*, 305–309.

Almeida, A. P. (2012) Can I ask a question? The importance of classroom questioning. *Procedia Social and Behavioral Sciences, 31*, 634–638.

Aschner, M. J. (1961). Asking questions to trigger thinking. *NEA Journal, 50*, 44–46.

Austin, J. (2000). Performance analysis and performance diagnostics. In J. Austin & J. E. Carr (Eds.), *Handbook of applied behavior analysis* (pp. 321–349). Reno, NV: Context Press.

Austin, J., Carr, J. E., & Agnew, J. L. (1999). The need for assessment of maintaining variables in OBM. *Journal of Organizational Behavior Management, 19*, 59–87.

Austin, J., Weatherly, N. L., & Gravina, N. E. (2005). Using task clarification, graphic feedback, and verbal feedback to increase closing-task completion in a privately owned restaurant. *Journal of Applied Behavior Analysis, 38*, 117–120.

Badiee, F., & Kaufman, D. (2014). Effectiveness of an online simulation for teacher education. *Journal of Technology and Teacher Education, 22*, 167–186.

Bandura, A. (1997). Self-efficacy: The exercise of control. New York, NY: W.H. Freeman.

Banks, J., Carson, J. S., Nelson, B. L., & Nicol, D. (2010). *Discrete-Event System Simulation* (5th ed.). Upper Saddle River, NJ: Prentice Hall.

Behavior Analyst Certification Board® Professional and Ethical Compliance Code for Behavior Analysts. Retrieved November 2, 2014, from Behavior Analyst Certification Board's website: https://www.bacb.com/wp-content/uploads/170706r_compliance_code_english.pdf

Béteille, T., Kalogrides, D., & Loeb, S. (2012). Stepping stones: Principal career paths and school outcomes. *Social Science Research 41*, 904–916.

Binder, C. (1996). Behavioral fluency: Evolution of a new paradigm. *The Behavior Analyst, 19*, 163–197.

Binder, C. (2003). Doesn't everybody need fluency? *Performance Improvement, 42*, 14–20.

Binder, C., & Watkins, C. L., (1990). Precision teaching and direct instruction: Measurably superior instructional technology in schools. *Performance Improvement Quarterly, 3*(4), 74–96.

Blase, J., & Blase, J. (2000). Effective instructional leadership: Teachers' perspectives on how principals promote teaching and learning in schools. *Journal of Educational Administration, 38*(2), 130–141.

Breaux, A., & Wong, H. (2003). *New teacher induction: How to train, support, and retain new teachers*. Mountain View, CA: Harry K. Wong Publications.

Brethower, D. M. (2002). Behavioral systems analysis: Fundamental concepts and cutting edge applications. Retrieved from http://www.behavior.org/resources/415.pdf

Bucklin, B. R., Dickinson, A. M., & Brethower, D. M. (2000). A comparison of the effects of fluency training and accuracy training on application and retention. *Performance Improvement Quarterly, 13*, 140–163.

Carr, J. E., Wilder, D. A., Majdalany, L., Mathisen, D., & Strain, L. A. (2013). An assessment-based solution to a human-service employee performance problem: An initial evaluation of the Performance Diagnostic Checklist—Human Services. *Behavior Analysis in Practice, 6*, 16–32.

Carroll, T. (2007). Policy brief: The high cost of teacher turnover. Retrieved from http://nctaf.org/wp-content/uploads/2012/01/NCTAF-Cost-of-Teacher-Turnover-2007-policy-brief.pdf

Carter, S. (2010). *The social validity manual: A guide to subjective evaluation of behavior interventions in applied behavior analysis*. London: Academic Press.

Cavanaugh, M. P., & Warwick, C. (2001). Questioning is an art. *Language Arts Journal of Michigan, 17*(2), 35–38.

Chartered Institute of Personnel and Development. (2018). Mentoring vs coaching table. Retrieved from https://www.cipd.co.uk/

Chin, C. (2007). Teacher questioning in science classrooms: Approaches that stimulate productive thinking. *Journal of Research in Science Teaching, 44*(6), 815–843.

Chin, C., & Osborne, J. (2008). Students' questions: A potential resource for teaching and learning science. *Studies in Science Education, 44*, 1–39.

Cooper, J., Heron, T., & Heward, W. (2007). *Applied behavior analysis*. Upper Saddle River, NJ: Pearson Education.

Cruickshank, D. (1988). The use of simulations in past, present, and future. *Simulation & Gaming 19*(2), 133–156.

Daniels, A., & Daniels, J. (2006). *Performance management: Changing behavior that drives organizational effectiveness*. Atlanta, GA: Performance Management Publications.

Darling-Hammond, L. (2006). Assessing teacher education: The usefulness of multiple measures for assessing program outcomes. *Journal of Teacher Education, 57*(2), 120–138.

de Bruin, A. B. H., Smits, N., Rikers, R. M. J. P., & Schmidt, H. G. (2008). Deliberate practice predicts performance over time in adolescent chess players and drop-outs: A linear mixed models analysis. *British Journal of Psychology, 99*, 473–497.

Doran, G. T. (1981). There's a S.M.A.R.T. way to write management's goals and objectives. *Management Review*. AMA FORUM. 70 (11): 35–36.

Duckworth, A. L., Peterson, C., Matthews, M. D., & Kelly, D. R. (2007). Grit: Perseverance and passion for long-term goals. *Journal of Personality and Social Psychology, 92*(6), 1087–1101.

Dweck, S. (2017). The journey to children's mindsets—and beyond. *Child Development Perspectives, 11*(2), 139.

Ellis, J., & Magee, S. (2007). Contingencies, macrocontingencies, and metacontingencies in current educational practices: No child left behind? *Behavior and Social Issues, 16*, 5–26.

Engelmann, S. (2007). Teaching needy kids in our backward system. Eugene, OR: ADI Press.

Erdem, F., & Aytemur, J. Ö. (2008). Mentoring—a relationship based on trust: Qualitative research. *Public Personnel Management, 37*(1), 55–65. Retrieved from https://search.proquest.com/docview/215934051?accountid=166077

Ericsson, K. A., Krampe, R. Th., & Tesch-Römer, C. (1993). The role of deliberate practice in the acquisition of expert performance. *Psychological Review, 100*(3), 363–406.

Ferguson, R. (2013). *Finally! Performance assessment that works: Big five performance management.* North Charleston, SC: CreateSpace.

Fox, E. J., & Ghezzi, P. M. (2003). Effects of computer-based fluency training on concept formation. *Journal of Behavioral Education, 12*, 1–21.

Fuqua, R. W., & Bosch, S. (2001). Behavioral cusps: A model for selecting target behaviors. *Journal of Applied Behavior Analysis, 34*, 123–125.

Gatheridge, B. (2005). Evaluation of behavioral skills training for teaching abduction prevention skills to young children. *Journal of Applied Behavior Analysis, 38*, 67–78.

Gavoni, P., & Edmonds, W. A. (2014). *Fight Psychology: I cud'a been a contenda Part 2: Skills from training to the fight.* http://www.scifighting.com/2014/06/03/29922/cud-contenda-part-2-generalization-skills-trainingfight/

Gavoni, P., & Rodriguez, M. (2016). *Quick wins! Accelerating school transformation through science, engagement, and leadership.* Melbourne, FL: ABA Technologies, Inc.

Geller, E. S. (2003). Should organizational behavior management expand its content? *Journal of Organizational Behavior Management, 22*(2), 13–30. doi:10.1300/J075v22n02_03

George, A. A., Hall, G. E., & Stiegelbauer, S. M. (2006). *Measuring implementation in schools: The Stages of Concern Questionnaire.* Austin, TX: SEDL. Available from http://www.sedl.org/pubs/catalog/items/cbam17.html

Glenn, S. (1991). Contingencies and metacontingencies: Relations among behavioral, cultural, and biological evolution. In P. A. Lamal (Ed.), *Behavioral analysis of societies and cultural practices* (pp. 39–73). New York, NY: Hemisphere Publishing Corporation.

Goldsmith, M., Lyons, L. S., & McArthur, S. (2000). *Coaching for leadership: How the world's greatest coaches help leaders learn.* San Francisco, CA: Jossey-Bass.

Goleman, D., Boyatzis, R., & McKee, A. (2002). *Primal leadership: Learning to lead with emotional intelligence.* Boston, MA: Harvard Business School Press.

Graesser, A., & Olde, (2003). How does one know whether a person understands a device? The quality of the questions the person asks when the device breaks down. *Journal of Educational Psychology, 95*, 524–536.

Gwande, A. (2010). *The checklist manifesto: How to get things right.* New York, NY: Metropolitan Books.

Hakanen, J. J., Bakker, A. B., & Schaufeli, W. B. (2006). Burnout and work engagement among teachers. *Journal of School Psychology, 43*, 495–513.

Harless, J. (2016). *The Eden Conspiracy: Educating for accomplished citizenship.* Reprinted from the 1998 edition with an Introduction and Epilogue by Carl Binder. Littleton, MA: The Cambridge Center for Behavioral Studies.

Hattie, J. (2009). *Visible learning: A synthesis of over 800 meta-analyses relating to achievement.* New York: Routledge.

Hornby, A., Turnbull, J., Lea, D., Parkinson, D., & Phillips, P. (2011). *Oxford advanced learner's dictionary of current English.* London: Oxford University Press.

Ingersoll, R., Merrill, L., & May, H. (2014). What are the effects of teacher education and preparation on beginning teacher attrition? (CPRE Research Report #RR-82). Philadelphia, PA: Consortium for Policy Research in Education. DOI:10.12698/cpre.2014.rr82

Jenkins, B., (2009). What it takes to be an instructional leader. *Principal*, 34–37. Retrieved from https://www.naesp.org/sites/default/files/J-F_p34.pdf

Jepson, E., & Forrest, S. (2006). Individual contributory factors in teacher stress: The role of achievement striving and occupational commitment. *British Journal of Educational Psychology, 76*, 183–197.

Johnson, D. A., Casella, S. E., McGee, H., & Lee, S. C. (2014). The use and validation of preintervention diagnostic tools in organizational behavior management. *Journal of Organizational Behavior Management, 34*, 104–121.

Johnson, D. A., & Rubin, S. (2011). Effectiveness of interactive computer-based instruction: A review of studies published between 1995 and 2007. *Journal of Organizational Behavior Management, 31*, 55–94.

Johnson, D. W., & Johnson, R.T. (1994). *Learning together and alone: Cooperative, competitive, and individualistic learning* (4th ed.). Boston, MA: Allyn & Bacon.

Johnson, K., & Layng, T. (1992). Breaking the structuralist barrier: Literacy and numeracy with fluency. *American Psychologist, 47*, 1475–1490.

Johnson, K., & Layng, T. (1994). The Morningside model of generative instruction. In R. Gardner, D. M. Sainato, J. O. Cooper, T. E. Heron, W. L. Heward, J. W. Eshleman, & T. Gross (Eds.). *Behavior analysis in education: Focus on measurably superior instruction* (pp. 173–197). Belmont, CA: Brooks/Cole.

Johnson, S., Cooper, C., Cartwright, S., Donald, I., Taylor, P., & Millet, C. (2005). The experience of work-related stress across occupations. *Journal of Managerial Psychology, 20*, 178–187.

Kagan, S., & Kagan, M. (2009). *Kagan Cooperative Learning.* San Clemente, CA: Kagan Publishing.

Klem, A. M., & Connell, J. P. (2004). Relationships matter: Linking teacher support to student engagement and achievement. *Journal of School Health, 74*(7), 262–273.

Knight, J. (Ed.) (2009). *Coaching: Approaches and perspectives.* Thousand Oaks, CA: Corwin Press.

Komaki, J., & Barnett, F. T. (1977). A behavioral approach to coaching football: Improving the play execution of the offensive backfield on a youth football team. *Journal of Applied Behavior Analysis, 10*, 657–664.

Laipple, J. (2012). *Rapid change: Immediate action for the impatient leader*. Atlanta, GA: Performance Management Publications.

Ledoux, S. F. (2014). *Running out of time: Introducing behaviorology to help solve global problems.* Ontario, Canada: BehaveTech Publishing.

Levine, A. (2005). *Educating school leaders.* Washington, DC: The Education Schools Project.

Lindsay, J., (2014). Direct instruction. Proven success in teaching. Retrieved from https://www.jefflindsay.com/EducData.shtml

Lippa, C. F. (2013). Loss of language skills in teachers: Is there a link to frontotemporal degeneration? *American Journal of Alzheimer's Disease and Other Dementias, 28*(6), 549. doi:10.1177/1533317513502251

Malott, M. (2003). *The paradox of organizational change. Engineering organizations with behavioral systems analysis.* Reno, NV: Context Press.

Marinell, W. H., & Coca, V. M. (2013). *Who stays and who leaves? Findings from a three part study of teacher turnover in NYC middle schools.* New York: The Research Alliance for NYC Schools.

Martin, G., & Hrycaiko, D. (1983). Effective behavioral coaching: What's it all about. *Journal of Sport and Exercise Psychology, 5,* 8–20.

Martinez-Onstott, B., Wilder, D., & Sigurdsson, S. (2016). Identifying the variable contributing to at-risk performance: Initial evaluation of the Performance Diagnostic Checklist-Safety (PDC-Safety). *Journal of Organizational Behavior Management, 36,* 80–93.

Marzano, R. J. (2007). *The art and science of teaching: A comprehensive framework for effective instruction.* Alexandria, VA: ASCD.

Marzano, R. J., Pickering, D. J., & Pollock, J. E. (2001). *Classroom instruction that works: Research-based strategies for increasing student achievement.* Alexandria, VA: Association for Supervision and Curriculum Development.

Maxwell, J. (2014). *Good leaders ask great questions: Your foundation for successful leadership.* New York, NY: Hatchette Book Group.

Megginson, D., & Clutterbuck, D. (2005). *Techniques for coaching and mentoring.* Amsterdam, Netherlands; London, England: Elsevier Butterworth-Heinemann.

Merrett, F. E., & Musgrove, W. J. (2010). The hierarchy of reinforcement: Mainspring of the behavioural approach to teaching and learning. *Educational Psychology, 2*(3–4), 301–312. doi:10.1080/0144341820020310

Miciano, R. (2004). Self-questioning and prose comprehension: A sample case of ESL reading. *Asia Pacific Education Review, 2*(3), 210–216.

Molenda, M., & Russell, J. D. (2006). Instruction as an intervention. In J. A. Pershing (Ed.), *Handbook of human performance technology* (pp. 335–369). San Francisco, CA: Pfeiffer.

Murphy, J., Moorman, H. N., & McCarthy, M. (2008). A framework for rebuilding initial certification and preparation programs in educational leadership: Lessons from whole-state reform initiatives. *Teachers College Record, 110,* 2172–2223.

Murphy, J., & Vriesenga, M. (2006). Research on school leadership preparation in the United States: An analysis. *School Leadership and Management, 26*(2), 183–195.

Naismith, J. (1941). *Basketball: Its origins and development.* Lincoln, NE: University of Nebraska Press.

Nelson-LeGall, S., & Glor-Scheib, S. (1985). Help-seeking in elementary classrooms: An observational study. *Contemporary Educational Psychology, 10,* 58–71.

Newman, F. (1992). *Student engagement and achievement in American secondary schools.* New York, NY: Teachers College Press.

No Child Left Behind Act of 2001, P.L. 107–110, 20 U.S.C. § 6319 (2002).

Redmon, W. K., & Mason, M. A. (2001). Organizational culture and behavioral systems analysis. In C. M. Johnson, W. K. Redmon, & T. C. Mawhinney (Eds.), *Handbook of organizational performance: Behavior analysis and management* (pp. 437–456). Binghamton, NY: The Haworth Press.

Reeves, D. (2000). Standards are not enough: Essential transformations for school success. *NASSP Bulletin, 84*(620), 5–19.

Reid, D., & Parsons, M. (2006). *Motivating human services staff: Supervisory strategies for maximizing work effort and work enjoyment.* Morganton, NC: Habilitative Management Consultants, Inc.

Rodriguez, M., Wilder, D. A., Therrien, K., Wine, B., Miranti, R., Daratany, K., … Rodriguez, M. (2005). Use of the Performance Diagnostic Checklist to select an intervention designed to increase the offering of promotional stamps at two sites of a restaurant franchise. *Journal of Organizational Behavior Management, 25,* 17–35.

Rosales-Ruiz, J., & Baer, D. M. (1997). Behavioral cusps: A developmental and pragmatic concept for behavior analysis. *Journal of Applied Behavior Analysis, 30*(3), 533–44.

Roth, W. M. (1996). Teacher questioning in an open-inquiry learning environment: Interactions of context, content, and student responses. *Journal of Research in Science Teaching, 33,* 709–736.

Sasson, J. R., Alvero, A. M., & Austin, J. (2006). Effects of process and human performance improvement strategies. *Journal of Organizational Behavior Management, 26*(3), 43–78. doi:10.1300/J075v26n03_02

Scheerens, J., Luyten, H., & van Ravens, J. (2011). Perspectives on educational quality: Illustrative outcomes on primary and secondary schooling in the Netherlands. Springer Briefs in Education. doi:10.1007/978-94-007-0926-3_2

School Leaders Network. (2014). Churn: The high cost of principal turnover. Retrieved from https://www.issuelab.org/resource/churn-the-high-cost-of-principal-turnover.html

Seashore Louis, K., Leithwood, K., Wahlstrom, K., & Anderson, S. (2010*). Investigating the links to improved student learning.* Washington, DC: Wallace Foundation.

Seniuk, H. A., Witts, B. N., Williams, W. L., & Ghezzi, P. M. (2013). On terms. *The Behavior Analyst, 36,* 167–172.

Shapiro, E. S., & Shapiro, S. (1985). Behavioral coaching in the development of skills in track. *Behavior Modification, 9,* 211–224.

Shook, G. L., Hartsfield, F., & Hemingway, M. (1995). Essential content for training behavior analysis practitioners. *The Behavior Analyst, 18,* 83–91.

Shook, G. L., Johnston, J. M., & Mellichamp, F. H. (2004). Determining essential content for applied behavior analyst practitioners. *The Behavior Analyst, 27,* 67–94.

Skinner, B. F. (1953). *Science and human behavior.* New York: The Free Press.

Skinner, B. F. (1984). The shame of American education. *American Psychologist, 39*(9), 947–954. http://dx.doi.org/10.1037/0003-066X.39.9.947

Sloan, M. C. (2010). Aristotle's Nicomachean Ethics as the original locus for the septem circumstantiae. *Classical Philology, 105,* 236–251.

Smith, T., & Ingersoll, R. (2004). What are the effects of induction and mentoring on beginning teacher turnover? *American Educational Research Journal (41)*3, 681–714.

Society for Human Resource Management. (2017). Coaching in a business environment. Retrieved from https://www.shrm.org/resourcesandtools/tools-and-samples/toolkits/pages/coachinginabusinessenvironment.aspx

Souza, B., (2015). *The weekly coaching conversation: A business fable about taking your team's performance—and your career—to the next level.* USA: Productivity Drivers, LLC.

Spillane, J., Halverson, R., & Diamond, J. (2001). Investigating school leadership practice: A distributed perspective. *Educational Researcher, 30*(3), 23–28. Published by American Educational Research Association.

Steiner, L., & Kowal, J. (2007, February). *Principal as instructional leader: Designing a coaching program that fits* (Issue Brief). Washington, DC: The Center for Comprehensive School Reform and Improvement.

Stürmer, K., Könings, K., & Seidel, T. (2012). Declarative knowledge and professional vision in teacher education: Effect of courses in teaching and learning. *British Journal of Educational Psychology, 83*(3), 467–483.

Sutcher, L., Darling-Hammond, L., & Carver-Thomas, D. (2016). A coming crisis in teaching? Teacher supply, demand, and shortages in the U.S. Palo Alto, CA: Learning Policy Institute. Retrieved from https://learningpolicyinstitute.org/product/coming-crisis-teaching

Tang, Y. Y., Tang, R., & Posner, M. (2013). Brief meditation training induces smoking reduction. *Proceedings of the National Academy of Sciences, 110* (34), 13971–13975.

Thompson, G. H., & Dass, P. (2000). Improving students' self-efficacy in strategic management: The relative impact of cases and simulations. *Simulation & Gaming, 31*(1), 22–41.

Tulgan, B. (1999). *FAST feedback* (2nd ed.). Amherst, MA: HRD Press, Inc.

US Department of Education. (2016). *Education Department releases final teacher preparation regulations.* Retrieved from https://www.ed.gov/news/press-releases/education-department-releases-final-teacher-preparation-regulations

Wallace Foundation. (2008). Becoming a leader: Preparing school principals for today's schools. Retrieved from https://www.wallacefoundation.org/knowledge-center/Documents/Becoming-a-Leader-Preparing-Principals-for-Todays-Schools.pdf

Walsh, K. (2006). Teacher education. Coming up empty. *Fwd 3*(1), 1–6.

Watkins, M. D. (2013). The first 90 days: Proven strategies for getting up to speed faster and smarter. Boston, MA: Harvard Business Review Press.

Weatherly, N. L. (in review). A behavioral safety model for clinical safety: Coaching for institutionalization. *Perspectives on Behavior Science.*

Wilder, D. A., Lipschultz, J. L., King, A., Driscoll, S., & Sigurdsson, S. (2018). An analysis of the commonality and type of preintervention assessment procedures in the Journal of Organizational Behavior Management (2000–2015). *Journal of Organizational Behavior Management, 38*, 5–17.

Wilen, W. (1991). *Questioning skills for teachers. What research says to the teacher* (3rd ed.). Washington, DC: National Education Association.

Wilson, C. (2007). *Best practice in performance coaching: A handbook for leaders, coaches, HR professionals and organizations.* Philadelphia, PA: Kogan Page Limited.

Wolf, M. M. (1978). Social validity: The case for subjective measurement or how applied behavior analysis is finding its heart. *Journal of Applied Behavior Analysis, 11*, 203–214.

ABOUT THE AUTHORS

Paul "Paulie" Gavoni, EdD, BCBA

With more than twenty years in human services and public education, Dr. Paul "Paulie" Gavoni has effectively translated research to practice through the application of evidenced-based strategies aimed at bringing out the best in children and adults. Recognized by many as an authentic leader, Paulie has provided coaching focused on analyzing and developing behavior and performance-management systems that positively impact student behavior and achievement in high-poverty schools.

An expert in human performance and organizational leadership, Paulie has passionately and directly supported students and staff in a variety of environments such as private schools, group homes, secured facilities, day-treatment programs, alternative education facilities, and public schools. Within these settings, Paulie has been fortunate enough to wear many hats, including professor, counselor, professional developer, case manager, therapist, behavior analyst, project manager, clinical coordinator, and school administrator.

Beyond his work in education and human services, Coach "Paulie Gloves" is also a highly successful professional mixed martial arts coach. As a former golden gloves heavyweight champion, Paulie successfully applies the science of human behavior to coach multiple fighters to championship titles at varying levels worldwide. With many successful fighters on his resume, Paul even helped one of his fighters reach the pinnacle of sport when he won and successfully defended the M-1 Global heavyweight title for three years. Paulie is a writer for Bloody Elbow, a featured coach in "Ring to Cage: How Four Former Boxers Help Mold MMA's Finest," and a featured coach in the book *Beast: Blood, Struggle, and Dreams at the Heart of Mixed Martial Arts.*

A frequent presenter at professional conferences, Paulie has presented across the country on topics related to coaching, leadership, professional development, and systems improvement in education.

Nicholas L. Weatherly, PhD, BCBA-D, LBA

nicweatherly.com

Dr. Nicholas Weatherly is a management consultant, an associate professor and chair of the Master of Arts program in Professional Behavior Analysis at Florida Institute of Technology's School of Behavior Analysis. His areas of teaching, research, and practice focus on developing sustainable business solutions, coaching systems, organizational assessments, and training systems. He has been invited to speak on these topics locally and internationally for over 15 years, giving or contributing to nearly 100 scholarly presentations and workshops. Prior to joining Florida Tech, Nic was a management consultant with Aubrey Daniels International where he led their instructional systems projects and consulted in a number of areas of business and industry including manufacturing, energy, banking, health insurance, and clinical services.

Nic is the Past-President of the Association of Professional Behavior Analysts and is also Past-President of both the Georgia Association for Behavior Analysis and the Kentucky Association for Behavior Analysis. He currently serves on the Editorial Board of the Journal of Organizational Behavior Management and continues to work on various workgroups and committees for the Behavior Analyst Certification Board, including serving as a member of the BACB Disciplinary Review Committee and currently as a Code Section Specialist for the BACB's Code Compliance Committee.

Nic has held advisory roles and served on the board of directors for a number of professional associations, advocacy groups, and service facilities including the New York State Association for Behavior Analysis, the Minnesota Northland Association for Behavior Analysis, and the Autism Treatment Association of Minnesota. He was the inaugural chair of the Kentucky Applied Behavior Analyst Licensing Board, one of the first stand-alone licensing boards for behavior analysis in the country, and continues to stay active in public policy efforts. He has also held full- and part-time academic appointments with a number of universities including St. Cloud State University, Western Michigan University, and the MBA Program at Regis University. Nic received his Ph.D. from Western Michigan University's Applied Behavior Analysis Program with concentrations on behavioral systems analysis, behavior-based safety, and programmed instruction. He is a Board Certified Behavior Analyst-Doctoral and licensed as a behavior analyst in Kentucky and Connecticut.

CPSIA information can be obtained
at www.ICGtesting.com
Printed in the USA
LVHW100319240919
631984LV00009B/392/P

9 781943 920372